Doing Veterans Oral History

By Barbara W. Sommer

A publication of the Oral History Association
in collaboration with the Library of Congress
Veterans History Project

ORAL HISTORY ASSOCIATION

VETERANS
HISTORY
PROJECT

About the Author

Barbara W. Sommer has over thirty-five years of experience in the oral history field. She has been principal investigator or director of a number of community oral history projects, has taught oral history, and has led many community and Veterans History Project workshops. Sommer is a long-time member of the Oral History Association (OHA) and is the author and co-author of several key publications in the field including *The Oral History Manual* (2nd edition 2009), *The American Indian Oral History Manual* (2008), the *Community Oral History Toolkit* (2013), and *Practicing Oral History in Historical Organizations* (2015). She holds degrees from Carleton College and the University of Minnesota.

About the OHA

Since 1967, the Oral History Association (OHA) has served as the principal membership organization for people committed to the value of oral history. OHA engages with policy makers, educators, and others to help foster best practices and encourage support for oral history and oral historians. With an international membership, OHA serves a broad and diverse audience including teachers, students, community historians, archivists, librarians, and filmmakers.

OHA encourages standards of excellence in the collection, preservation, dissemination and uses of oral testimony. OHA has established the *Principles and Best Practices*—a set of goals, guidelines, and evaluation standards for oral history interviews. The OHA pamphlet series offers basic and useful information about planning, conducting, interpreting, processing, and publishing oral history programs and projects.

For more information about OHA, contact the Oral History Association at Georgia State University, P.O. Box 4117, Atlanta, GA 30302-4117. Email: oha@gsu.edu. Website: http://www.oralhistory.org/

Cover photos clockwise from top left:
Elvin E. Thomas Collection (AFC 2001/001/33621); **Mary L. Weiss Hester Collection** (AFC/2001/001/32449); **Larry Schwab Collection** (AFC/2001/001/23979); Participants at a Veterans History Project workshop co-hosted with Senator Joe Donnelly (IN), Hamilton East Public Library, Fishers, IN; **Joseph Arden Beimfohr Collection** (AFC/2001/001/54904). Photos courtesy of Veterans History Project, American Folklife Center, Library of Congress.

ISBN-13
978-0-9845947-3-3

Oral histories with veterans are some of the most commonly done interviews today. With support from the Library of Congress Veterans History Project, along with the work of many organizations and institutions throughout the United States, interviews are being recorded with veterans from all wars and conflicts as well as those who served in peacetime and those who were in support positions. Veterans and non-veterans, family members and those who do not know the veterans except through an interview—all are participating in this effort, as are students from many grade levels and post-secondary institutions. Veterans and interviewers, working together, are helping preserve the veterans' memories. Their information, preserved and made accessible, is recorded in the voices of individuals who were part of national and international events that shaped our history.

This pamphlet is the result of collaboration between the Oral History Association (OHA), the principal organization for people working with oral histories, and the Veterans History Project of the Library of Congress. Oral historians work to a set of legal and ethical standards. Information in the pamphlet applies these standards, as stated in the OHA *Principles and Best Practices*, to interviews with veterans.

The pamphlet begins with an overview of oral history. This chapter includes background on the basics and introduces the interview process. It is followed by chapters describing the interview process in detail. Before-Interview tasks, including selecting a veteran to interview, doing background research, and preparing interview questions, are first. The Interview, the central piece of the oral history process, is covered next. Included here are tips on conducting an interview and suggestions for working with veterans in a variety of situations. After-Interview steps complete the process.

The next section of the pamphlet presents guidelines for doing interviews with veterans in secondary and post-secondary settings. It also is based on the standard methodology, but includes information specific to interviewing veterans in the classroom. It is followed by a chapter providing examples of recommended resources for use when interviewing veterans and, at the end, by an appendix containing additional information and examples of forms and other materials that can be useful as well.

The oral history process described in this pamphlet takes time but pays off in the quality of the interviews. Understanding the limits on the time of both interviewers and veterans, it is suggested the process be followed as closely as possible.

Thank you to everyone who contributes the time and energy to recording the stories and memories of our veterans.

ACKNOWLEDGMENTS

This publication in the Oral History Association (OHA) pamphlet series is written for the many people, often volunteers, who give their time and effort to record and preserve the memories of veterans. First, thank you to Cliff Kuhn, Executive Director of the Oral History Association, and Monica Mohindra, Head, Program Coordination and Communication, Veterans History Project, Library of Congress, for their strong support in developing this pamphlet.

Thank you also to Fiona Anthes, Jo Blatti, Ellen Brooks, Emily Carley, Jeff D. Corrigan, Cynthia Macauley, Sarah Milligan, Paul Ortiz, Mary Kay Quinlan, Sharon D. Raynor, Troy Reeves, Sue VerHoef, and Bob Wettemann for valuable input and information. Each of you contributed knowledge and insight about your own experiences in interviewing veterans that added greatly to the information presented in this pamphlet And thank you to Jeanne Barker-Nunn, whose thoughtful edits helped strengthen the manuscript.

"Sitting down to reflect on that period in my life was a powerful—and rewarding—experience. I'd like to encourage other veterans across the country to join me in recording their own stories so that our children and grandchildren may have the opportunity to hear about these important moments in American history."

—**William D. Adams**, Chairman of the National Endowment for the Humanities (NEH), commenting on recording an interview about his service in the United States Army for the Library of Congress Veterans History Project. http://www.neh.gov/news/press-release/2015-05-21

Participants at a Veterans History Project workshop co-hosted with Senator Joe Donnelly (IN), Hamilton East Public Library, Fishers, IN.

TABLE OF CONTENTS

Chapter 1

Introduction to Oral History.. 3

Chapter 2

Before the Interview... 13

The Interview 36

After the Interview... 57

Chapter 3

Secondary and Post-Secondary Education........................... 63

Appendices..79

Staff Sergeant Elvin E. Thomas
  Elvin E. Thomas Collection (AFC 2001/001/33621), Veterans History Project, American Folklife Center, Library
  of Congress

1 AN INTRODUCTION TO ORAL HISTORY

Many of us remember stories we've heard over the years—accounts of our families and how we came to be where we are and who we are. Maybe they were our family's immigration stories or stories of the working lives of our family members. Maybe they were stories of our communities or of the Great Depression passed down in our families. And maybe they were stories of our veterans and their experiences in their service to our country. As we listened to these stories, whether they were easy or difficult to hear, they helped ground us. They gave us a sense of individual and family identity. But stories can do more than that. They also give us first-hand accounts of past times and events and help link us to them. They help us remember that our individual stories are part of the greater whole of our shared history. This pamphlet on recording oral histories with veterans is designed to offer the tools to preserve their stories and make them accessible as part of our shared history.

American Veterans

A veteran is a person of any rank who has served for any length of time in any branch of the military service. This includes all branches of the Armed Forces—Army, Navy, Marines, Air Force, Coast Guard, Merchant Marine, National Guard, and the Reserves. Others whose stories often are included in veterans' projects are individuals who served in support of a United State war or conflict in a professional capacity, such as war industry workers, USO personnel, flight instructors, and medical workers. For purposes of this pamphlet, they are included here.

According to official figures, there are almost twenty-two million military veterans in the United States today. They include veterans of all wars and of peacetime military service and represent men and women of all ethnic groups and backgrounds. About another 1.2 million people are currently serving in the United States Armed Forces. Although the figure can vary by age, about 60 percent of all Americans have immediate family members who have served or are currently serving in the military.[1] When including extended family and support personnel, the numbers go even higher. The impact of this large number of current and past members of the armed services and related service personnel on our population is great; their stories and memories can add immeasurably to our understanding of the events and times which they experienced first-hand.

Veterans' memories, like their experiences, are quite diverse. There are veterans who enlisted and others who were drafted. Veterans have served overseas and at home. Some have served in combat, some in combat support positions, and some did not see combat at all. They include both officers and enlisted personnel in all branches of the Service. Their experiences range from daily routines to the extreme stress of combat. They may have memories of training, assignments, friendships, battles, wars, service at home and abroad, and the challenges of reintegrating into civilian life after their time in the military. Each veteran has a unique story, but all are part of our history.

Oral History

Oral history is the collection, preservation, and interpretation of firsthand experiences about the past recorded in interview form. It offers a personal perspective on history from people whose voices often otherwise might not be included in the historical record. An oral history—the term refers both to the process and the product—is the result of the interaction between an interviewer and a narrator. Both roles are important in the oral history process. The interviewer sets up and prepares for the interview and asks questions designed to yield fruitful responses. The narrator describes his or her experiences and gives them meaning and context.

The goal in recording an oral history interview is to provide as full an accounting of a narrator's information and experiences as possible, in his or her own words. Through use of open-ended and follow-up questions, interviewers strive to create interviews with depth and nuance that go beyond the basic facts of a person's story. Such interviews illustrate the strength of oral history—that an exchange between interviewer and narrator can add new and powerful voices to the historical record. An oral history interview also provides an opportunity for narrators to put their personal experiences into a larger perspective. With guidance from trained and prepared interviewers and the understanding that the purpose of oral history is to document history through the memories of individuals, oral history interviews give narrators an opportunity to discuss their personal experiences and reflect on their meaning.

How people tell their stories can be as significant as the facts that they recall. In *The Things They Carried*, author and Vietnam veteran Tim O'Brien wrote of "happening-truth" and "story-truth" memories. As described by oral historian Kim Heikkila in *Sisterhood of War: Minnesota Women in Vietnam*, happening-truth is the literal truth, while story-truth is the emotional truth. Both truths are important parts of the interview process, and both can be part of an interview. Learning to listen for, recognize, and discuss both factual information and experiences and their meanings is part of the interviewing process.[2]

Generally, oral history interviews involve two people—the narrator and the interviewer:

- The narrator is someone with firsthand knowledge about the interview topic and the ability to communicate that information.

- The interviewer carries the responsibility for conducting the interview. This person is in charge of doing background research, developing topics and questions, scheduling the interview, conducting the interview, and taking care of follow-up tasks. Also important to being an effective interviewer is an understanding of oral history ethics and the ability to build a relationship of trust with the narrator.

The oral history interview process has three major stages—before the interview, during the interview, and after the interview. Briefly introduced here, each of these three major parts is covered in more detail in the following chapters.

An Integrated Series of Steps

The stage before an oral history interview involves research, information-gathering, and preparation by both participants. For the narrator, this stage includes agreeing to be interviewed and to take the time to provide the interviewer with information to help with interview preparation. For the interviewer, the time commitment at this stage is more extensive. It involves doing some background research, scheduling the interview, checking the equipment, preparing topics and questions, and preparing the legal release agreement to cover copyright ownership of the interview information.

Before the Interview

Background research is a necessary step in preparing for an interview. It includes gathering information from the narrator before the interview—such as where and when she served in the military, the branch of the Service he was in, the type of training he received, when she left the Service—that can suggest options for further research and review. This research in turn helps the interviewer structure the interview guide—the set of topics and questions the interviewer uses when interviewing the narrator.

Because oral histories are copyrightable documents, copyright law dictates that legal release agreements must be used to clarify who owns rights to the interview. Therefore, developing a release form is another activity that takes place before the interview. This often is done with the help of a repository—a permanent place where it will be kept and made accessible to users of the interview. Oral histories need ongoing care to preserve them and make them accessible on a long-term basis. Finding a repository to provide this care and ensure the oral history remains accessible can take time, but it is a necessary step. The repository that agrees to take the oral history helps develop the legal release agreement and is named in it.

Modern oral history is a recording equipment–based process, and decisions about the type of equipment to use and an understanding of how to operate it also are part of the before-interview process. Technology has advanced from early use of wire recorders to today's digital recorders, but the intention remains the same—to record and preserve interviews for future users.

Identifying and reviewing a location for the interview is another before-interview task. This includes checking that the location is readily accessible and has a good recording environment.

These before-interview steps are critical parts of the interview process. Taken together, they help lay the foundation for an interview.

During the Interview

The interview is the heart of the oral history process. It is the information-gathering session that preserves memories and helps add new voices to the historical record.

An oral history interview often consists of several parts: (1) a standard introduction, (2) introductory questions that typically focus on the narrator's personal background, (3) content questions that concentrate on the narrator's information about the interview topics, and (4) reflection questions.

Oral history interviewers use open-ended questions and follow-up questions. Follow-up questions help define details of the narrator's answers to the open-ended questions.

Interactions between the interviewer and narrator in an oral history interview comply with a recognized set of ethics and an understanding of best practices. Trust between the narrator and interviewer is an important part of this process; it often develops as a result of the before-interview preparations and the signals that these preparations send to a narrator about the importance of his information.

Interviews take time. They begin with the before-interview preparations and end with the after-interview tasks. A recording session may last from a half hour to many hours in length, but the time spent before and after the recording session also is critical to the end result. It is helpful for interviewers to be aware of this when agreeing to do an interview.

Oral historians are aware that interviews are most vulnerable to damage or loss between the end of the interview and the time they are sent to the designated repository. Thus, they take several after-interview steps to protect an interview and make sure it is preserved and accessible to future users.

After the Interview

After-interview steps include making copies of the recording, developing or helping develop such access materials as a transcript and information for online access tools, writing a thank-you letter to the narrator, and sending all the interview materials to the repository. Interviewers often make a copy of the recording and transcript as a gift for the narrator and send it as well.

The ethical framework that should be followed in oral history interviews is based on respect for the narrator. Full transparency is an oral history best practice. This involves being clear about the purpose of the interview and the reasons for choosing the veteran as narrator. Transparency also includes informing the narrator about the final disposition of the interview—where it will be permanently held and how its contents will be shared with others into the future. Ethical oral historians will be careful not to make promises they cannot keep.

Ethical Issues in Oral History

Taking the time to prepare for an interview is another oral history ethical best practice. An interviewer who makes an effort to learn about a narrator's background honors the narrator.

Trust between an interviewer and narrator is an important part of the interview process. A narrator who can see that an interviewer has come prepared for an interview and is open and honest in answering questions about the interview process often will be more willing to be interviewed.

Understanding this situation and handling it honestly with the narrator is another important ethical practice, as a narrator relies on the interviewer to guide the interview according to oral history ethics and best practices.

The Oral History Association (OHA) *Principles and Best Practices* are helpful guides to the ethical practice of oral history (http://www. oralhistory.org/about/principles-and-practices/). They can provide a framework for ethical and respectful interaction between interviewers and narrators and for defining boundaries and setting standards. Familiarity with the guides shows respect for the narrator which can help build trust between narrator and interviewer.

And finally, if a potential narrator refuses to be interviewed or to have the interview shared once it has been conducted, that decision must be respected. Veterans or anyone else should never be recorded in secret or tricked into telling their stories on a recording.

Legal Issues in Oral History

The copyright for the information recorded in an oral history interview is held by those who participated in it unless they explicitly transfer it in writing. Oral historians use a legal release agreement to clarify oral history copyright and to guide ongoing preservation and access to an interview. The release forms are signed by the narrator and interviewer at the end of an interview; if multiple interviews are conducted with the same person, a new form is signed after each interview. See Appendix B for an example of a legal release agreement transferring copyright to a designated repository, a common form of legal release agreement.[4]

In rare cases, interviewers may bring up information that needs special attention, such as a description of an illegal action. If this is the case, identified either in the before-interview discussion or during the interview, check with a knowledgeable person to determine how to proceed.

Repository

Determining a repository for an oral history is a critical step in planning for its preservation and access. Interviews with veterans often are intended to go to an archive, such as the Veterans History Project at the Library of Congress, but the interviewer should make sure this decision is clarified with both the narrator and the repository as early as possible. A narrator may want an interview to be given to a specific place and a repository may have specific equipment requirements or legal release agreement language that needs to be followed. Learning about these needs in advance can help keep the oral history process moving along smoothly. Identifying a repository also helps ensure long-term access to the oral history interview.

Equipment

Oral histories are recorded documents. Which audio and video recording equipment an interviewer decides to use can vary depending on the needs of the interview, the requirements of the repository, and the wishes of the narrator. The *Best Practices for Community Oral Historians* states that when recording an interview, interviewers should choose appropriate technology with an eye to both present and future needs.[5]

Oral history basics emphasize the use of good equipment for recording voices, the use of an external microphone if possible, and the option to record in an uncompressed recording format for audio and the least compressed recording format possible for video. The goal is a high-quality recording that can stand the test of time as much as currently possible.[6]

A decision on whether to use audio recording equipment, video recording equipment, or both is one that should be made for each interview. If the narrator knows an interview will contain a visual component such as use of photographs or a particular setting that can benefit from video, the interview should be video recorded. If an interview does not contain visual elements or the narrator is not willing to be video recorded, the interview should be audio recorded. Audio and video recording will both pick up unspoken communications, but those communications can be easier to see and interpret on video; this provides additional information but also could also feel intrusive for some veterans.

Selecting a recording format also involves decisions. Repositories often have lists of what recording formats they will accept. The Veterans History Project, for example, provides a list of acceptable audio and video formats that includes several analog formats and a number of common digital formats. Standard uncompressed digital audio (.wav, for example) is recommended for audio. Common compressed video formats are useful for recording and access purposes.

The best advice is to carefully check all equipment options. Don't feel bound by any one option; look everything over and decide what is best for each individual situation. See Appendix E for additional equipment guidelines.

Although there is no single formula for doing a good interview, practices in each stage of the oral history process serve as standards and guidelines for high-quality interviews. The Oral History Association *Principles and Best Practices* (http://www.oralhistory.org/about/principles-and-practices/) define oral history ethics and describe a process that sets oral history apart from other forms of interviewing, covering such topics as the following:

Oral History Best Practices

- The importance of obtaining informed consent, which means that all participants in an interview understand its purpose and final disposition.

- Ethical and legal concerns, including use of the release form.

- Sensitivity to issues of preservation and access, including their impact on the choice of a recorder.

- The importance of open and transparent communication among all interview participants at all times.

Central to the excitement and satisfaction of the oral history process is the vibrancy of the interview, the understanding that results from recording memories that may never have been spoken before, and the knowledge that the information recorded by the interviewer and narrator will become part of an ongoing record from which others can learn. OHA *Principles and Best Practices* remind us that the ethical practice of oral history is central to every part of this process. The next chapters describe the process in more detail.

References

[1.] *The Military-Civilian Gap: Fewer Family Connections*, Pew Research Center Social and Demographic Trends, November 23, 2011, http://www.pewsocialtrends.org/2011/11/23/the-military-civilian-gap-fewer-family-connections/, accessed August 7, 2015.

[2.] Tim O'Brien, *The Things They Carried* (New York, NY: Houghton Mifflin Harcourt), 171. Kim Heikkila, *Sisterhood of War: Minnesota Women in Vietnam* (St. Paul: Minnesota Historical Society Press, 2011),12.

[3.] Mary Kay Quinlan, Nancy MacKay, Barbara W. Sommer, *Interviewing in Community Oral History: Community Oral History Toolkit*, Volume 4. (Walnut Creek, CA: Left Coast Press, Inc. 2013), 27.

[4.] Additional copyright options are use of public domain or Creative Commons attribution. For more information, see John Neuenschwander, *A Guide to Oral History and the Law* (New York, NY: Oxford University Press, 2014). See also Barbara W. Sommer, *Practicing Oral History in Historical Organizations* (Walnut Creek, CA: Left Coast Press, Inc. 2015).

[5.] Mary Kay Quinlan, Nancy MacKay, and Barbara W. Sommer, *Introduction to Community Oral History: Community Oral History Toolkit*, Volume 1. (Walnut Creek, CA: Left Coast Press, Inc., 2013),12-13.

[6.] For up-to-date information about oral history recording equipment, see *Oral History in the Digital Age,* http://ohda.matrix.msu.edu, accessed July 17, 2015. See also Barbara W. Sommer, Nancy MacKay, and Mary Kay Quinlan, "Recording Equipment Standards," *Planning A Community Oral History Project: Community Oral History Toolkit*, Volume 2. (Walnut Creek, CA: Left Coast Press, Inc., 2013), 119-124.

Wilma and Staff Sergeant Kenje Ogata
Kenje Ogata Collection (AFC/2001/001/30983), Veterans History Project,
American Folklife Center, Library of Congress

2 THE INTERVIEW

Before the Interview

Oral history interviews begin before the narrator and interviewer sit down together to record the interview and continue after the recorder is turned off. This section of the pamphlet explains the before-interview steps.

Speaking from experience, Stephanie George, archivist at the Center for Oral and Public History at California State University-Fullerton, wrote of the Center's El Toro Marine Corps Air Station Oral History Project that, "there's a mindset … that suggests oral history is simply taking a recorder into the field and spending a few hours with someone. On the contrary, helping interviewers understand 'their' role … (is) a real challenge."[1] As she describes, the interview process is a longer one than just the interviewer's time with a narrator and recorder. It begins with the interviewer's decision to participate in the project and the clarification of what to expect. The commitment to follow the recommended steps from beginning to end helps honor a veteran's story.

Oral historians often find that people who haven't previously talked much about their memories become ready to do so at certain times in their lives or under certain circumstances. This can be especially true for veterans, many of whom may have stayed silent about their experiences for years. Veterans sometimes worry, however, that if they talk about their memories, others may not fully understand or may negatively judge their experiences. Anyone interviewing a veteran will want to remember that it often takes a great deal of courage for veterans to tell their stories. It also takes a great deal of courage for many veterans to include or allow their emotions—the depth of feelings generated by the memories—to be part of the telling of their stories.

The Interviewer

An oral history interviewer guides the interview. This person is responsible for making the commitment to do the interview and then seeing it through all the stages. Basically, after a veteran has agreed to be interviewed, the interviewer's before-interview tasks are as follows:

- Define the purpose of the interview and begin making a connection with the narrator.

- Do background research and prepare an interview guide.

- Decide on recording equipment and practice using it.

- Confirm the availability of a repository for the interview.

- Review all forms, including the legal release agreement, and make sure all are ready for use in the interview.

- Schedule the interview.

Some interviews involve an interviewing team to share these duties. If this is the case, the team often includes an equipment operator and a note-taker. The equipment operator handles the recording equipment and the note-taker helps the interviewer with logistics such as setting up the interview. All can help with many of the other tasks including background research, identifying a repository, reviewing the forms, and developing the question guide.

The Narrator

Interviewers frequently approach an interview either seeking the name of a narrator from a list supplied by a veterans group, historical society or another organization, or with a particular narrator already in mind. Many interviews begin because the interviewer has a personal connection to the narrator. Wanting to know and preserve a specific person's story often is the primary motivation for the interview. The interviewer or someone close to the narrator also may realize a narrator is one of the few remaining people with firsthand memories of a time, place, or event that should be preserved. Or maybe the interviewer is aware that a narrator is the person most able to communicate that information. These motivations are a good starting point for an interviewer when considering doing an interview.

Veterans as Narrators

Wars and conflicts are part of our history. Historians, studying them, often look for what can be learned about their causes, battles, and outcomes. Veterans as narrators have compelling and unique individual stories that can contribute to this knowledge. They remember details about life in a combat zone or days spent at a remote missile site during the Cold War. These stories, while personal, fit within this national and international narrative and help us put a personal face on it.

When looking for veterans to interview, keep several characteristics in mind. The first of these is a willingness to be interviewed. Also seek out people who have clear firsthand memories of the events to be discussed and can take time with an interviewer to talk about them. Make sure a narrator is capable of understanding why he or she is being asked to be interviewed and what will happen to their interviews after they are recorded. And ensure that the veteran understands the purpose and wording of the legal release agreement and the need for his or her, and the interviewer's, signatures on the agreement after the interview. In oral history terms, these understandings are referred to as informed consent and interview ethics. They require that the interviewer has made sure that the narrator understands the interview process and the purpose of the interview.

Choosing a Veteran as a Narrator

Suggestions about veterans who might be interviewed can come from many sources. Names are put forward by friends or acquaintances, from family members, and from veterans themselves. Veterans' groups and historical organizations such as veterans' museums also are good sources to turn to for identifying possible narrators; they often know the communities and may keep general lists of people willing to be interviewed. Oral historian Sharon Raynor describes such groups or institutions as community partners. Their members, when they understand the purpose and value of the interview process can become an interviewer's or project's strongest local allies in identifying or recruiting narrators.[2]

There are many reasons to consider interviewing a particular veteran. Maybe a veteran's family members want to know more about his experiences and how they have shaped his life. Maybe neighbors or friends want to support or honor someone they know. Community organizations may want to organize a set of interviews with local veterans as civic projects, or historical organizations may want to add more first-person information to their collections.

When asked to do an oral history interview, the request may surprise a veteran; many have kept their experiences to themselves for decades. Their reactions can run the gamut from being enthusiastic to being suspicious or concerned to even being afraid about taking part in an interview. Some veterans may see their participation as part of an important process of helping people understand what can be learned from their experiences. Others may hold back, perhaps willing to talk about some memories but not others, or they may be worried about being asked questions that are too painful to answer And there are some who, in what has been described as the "profound silence" of veterans, won't or can't talk about their experiences, or may simply prefer forgetting to remembering.[3] Even with their unique knowledge, it is a veteran's decision to be interviewed.

As with many narrators, the timing of the request for an interview with a veteran can often make a difference. Generally, veterans become more ready to talk about their experiences in their later years. Many veterans of World War II, the Korean War, the Vietnam War, and the Cold War have now reached a time in their lives when they may be ready to break their long silences with an interview. Yet some interviewers have also noticed that, breaking with this established pattern, many veterans of recent conflicts are willing to talk about their experiences relatively recently after the end of their assignments and may more readily agree to requests for interviews at a younger age than previous generations of veterans.

Sharing information about what will happen to an interview is important when conducting oral histories, but this can take on added significance when interviewing veterans. In oral histories, personal, private, and sometimes intense memories eventually become public as recorded interviews become research documents. For many veterans, this is okay; for some it is not. But each veteran asked to do an interview should understand what is being asked of him and why.

When thinking about an interview, interviewers or project directors will want to consider carefully the appropriateness or effectiveness of pairing particular interviewers and narrators. Pairing people who are likely to build a trust relationship and complete an in-depth and informative interview is an important step in the oral history process. Understanding that not every interviewer will have a choice among possible narrators, the examples here offer guidelines for different kinds of possible interviewer/narrator pairs when interviewing veterans.

Interviewer-Narrator Pairs

Many experts in conducting veterans' oral histories suggest that interviewers who are veterans be paired with veteran narrators if possible. The reasoning here is that their shared experience can lead to a more insightful and complex interview. An interviewer who shares experiences with the veteran is likely to know more about what to ask and how to ask it, even if the interviewer did not serve in the same branch of the Service or at the same time as the veteran. As oral historian Sue VerHoef has said, "When a veteran knows that the person asking the questions has seen it and understands, it creates a safe place. The interview atmosphere is: 'There is nothing I can say that will shock someone or make them think less of me. They get it.'"[4]

Veteran/Veteran Pair

A shared understanding is important, but even with this pairing, interviewers will want to be sensitive to factors which can have an impact on the interview. A shared experience could result in the interviewer inserting his own observations or thoughts into the discussion. Interviewers sometimes do this in an effort to make a narrator feel more comfortable, but, instead of helping the narrator, this can be off-putting and can have an adverse effect on the interview. A shared experience also could make the interview more difficult for a veteran interviewer if the intensity of those memories derails an interview or moves its focus away from the narrator's information. Service rank may also be a factor; pairing an interviewer and narrator of significantly different ranks could possibly affect an interview. Another consideration is that people with shared experiences sometimes talk in a shorthand that may not be clear to other people; veterans serving as interviewers will want to remember to take a step back and ask questions as if they don't already know the answers or understand the military jargon being used.

Veteran/veteran pairings of interviews and narrators often work very well. But as with any oral history interviewer/narrator pairing, consideration of the many factors at play can help produce a strong interview.

Veteran/Non-Veteran Pair

Thoughtful pairing of a veteran and non-veteran interviewer and narrator also can work well. The positives in this case include the lack of firsthand knowledge that an interviewer brings to an interview, which can lead to asking questions that other non-veterans will be interested in and that veterans may take for granted or assume is clear. An interviewer's openness to listening to often-told information, which they are hearing for the first time, can help stimulate a veteran's discussion of his experiences. A veteran may appreciate being able to talk with someone who does not share her background but is genuinely interested in learning about her experiences—for example, what she did before entering the Armed Forces and what some of the important or turning points were in her life during or after leaving the Service. These considerations can help produce a strong interview with a veteran/non-veteran pair.

Other Considerations for Interviewer/ Narrator Pairs

In addition to considering whether to pair a veteran narrator with a veteran or non-veteran interviewer, there are other considerations that can have an impact on how effective the pairs may be. These include differences or similarities in age, gender, religion, ethnic background, educational background, political background, or geographic background. Some veterans may prefer being interviewed by members of their own cultural or ethnic group. Some women may prefer being interviewed by a woman, and some men may prefer being interviewed by a man. As noted earlier, differences in military rank can have an impact on how the pairing functions, as can the age of the interviewer and narrator. Perhaps the most important thing to keep in mind is that for oral history interviewers, there are pluses and minuses both to being an outsider and being an insider. The ability of an interviewer to build a relationship with a narrator that is based on trust and rapport is a key factor to consider when pairing a veteran and an interviewer.

Group Interviews

Oral historians sometimes are asked about the advisability of doing group interviews in which people who often have known one another for a long time and traded stories about a particular event or time sit down together to be interviewed. A decision on whether to conduct this type of interview depends on the stated purpose of the interview. If it is intended to record the stories and the interactions of the people telling them, a group interview can be a workable approach and one in which the participants can help prompt one another. If, however, the purpose of the interview is to document an individual's memories, a one-on-one interview is probably preferable. A one-on-one interview gives a narrator the time to tell his unique story and for a narrator and interviewer to explore the meanings and depth of the narrator's memories.

A number of other issues also need to be considered when doing a group interview. One is the role of the interviewer. In a group interview, the interviewer can become more of a moderator, asking about certain stories but not following up with probing questions in the same way as in a one-on-one interview. The choice of interview topics also may be a point to consider; the interviewer will want to make sure that all members of the group are clear about and comfortable with the topics to be covered and the stories to be told. Clarifying who is talking in the recorded version can be a challenge in group interviews, even with the use of video. And specifications from repositories also are a factor; not all repositories accept group interviews. If an interviewer decides to do a group interview, careful attention to details such as these can help make it run smoothly and support its ongoing preservation and access.

Interviewing Families of Veterans

Although oral history interviews with veterans typically focus on their experiences in military service or military support positions, they may also focus on related topics such as homefront activities. Another area that interests some interviewers is the experience of family members of veterans. Interviewers may want to document what it was like to be at home while the veteran was deployed far away or what the reintegration process was like when the veteran returned home. An interview might focus on the experiences of family members who care for wounded and disabled veterans. Interviews such as these, though the veteran is not the narrator, can expand available information about veterans' experiences. Care must be taken to respect both the narrator's story and the veteran's experiences when contemplating these interviews. Interviewers can apply the recommendations in this pamphlet—with emphasis on a thorough understanding of oral history ethics and sensitivity to all involved— when conducting interviews with family members of veterans, but before beginning the interview process, should check with the repository. Many veterans' museums and collections will not accept interviews with family members. Some, such as the Veterans History Project, although not accepting the interviews, provide lists of other repositories that collect veteran's materials (http://www.loc.gov/vets/scope.html). Contact with a repository about its collecting policy before doing an interview with a family member can be a help to all involved.

Interviewer
Preparation

Interview preparation is an important part of the interview process. Although it takes time, it is not difficult and will pay off in the interview.

Interviewers working with veterans, whether experienced or new to the process, volunteers or paid staff, can benefit from interviewer training to orient them to the process and to considerations specific to working with veterans. State historical societies, local historical organizations, oral history centers at colleges and universities, the Oral History Association, regional oral history associations, and the Library of Congress Veterans History Project all offer training sessions at various times and locales. Check with each to find out about offerings in your area.

Interviewing workshops usually include examples of support materials designed for use when doing interviews. These are the forms and correspondence that an interviewer needs for an interview. The most common forms are the following; the examples here have been modified for use with veteran narrators:

Legal Release Agreement. This form identifies ownership of the interview information for copyright purposes. It is a key oral history form.

Biographical Data Form. Interviewers use this form to compile information about the narrator. The form documents information about the life or career of the narrator and often is the starting place for interview preparation and research.

Interview Summary Form. Interviewers use this form to summarize interview content. It is part of the after-interview process and helps guide ongoing use of the interview information.

Photograph/Memorabilia/Artifact Form. This form is used when a narrator discusses photographs, memorabilia such as cards or letters from home, or artifacts such as medals and uniforms. It is a tool to help the interviewer keep track of these items if they are mentioned in the interview.

The types of correspondence that interviewers can use in their written communications with narrators and institution often include the following:

Interview Contact. This letter formally requests that a narrator participate in an interview.

Interview Confirmation. This letter confirms the time and date of the interview and provides the narrator with information about the interview process.

Thank you. With this letter, the interviewer thanks the narrator for the interview. A copy of the interview often is sent with the letter.

Transmittal. The interviewer uses this letter when sending the oral history materials to the repository.

See Appendices B, C, and D for examples of these items.

The First Step

As with many oral histories, the motivation for conducting interviews with veterans is usually a desire by an interviewer, a veteran, or a sponsoring organization or institution not to lose a piece of history. Oral history best practices remind us, however, that the decision to record an oral history interview with a veteran, even with the best motivations or desires, should be founded on a clear understanding of what is expected from everyone involved. As oral historian Sarah Milligan recommends, "Be focused and intentional about what you want to discuss in an interview and why, and be focused and intentional about who you want to interview and why."[6] This means thoroughly thinking through the purpose for doing the interview.

Statement of Purpose

To define the purpose of an interview, an interviewer should answer two important questions: why interview this narrator at this time and place about this information, and what are the most important pieces of information to cover during the interview? A helpful way to begin to think through the answers to these questions can be to write a short statement of purpose. A statement of purpose doesn't need to be detailed, but it should be specific about why the narrator is being asked to be interviewed. A few examples of purpose statements are the following:

- To document the experience of a soldier participating in Operation Desert Storm in January 1991.

- To document the experience of a nurse in a Mobile Army Surgical Hospital (MASH) unit in Vietnam in 1966.

- To document the experience of a worker at a Minuteman missile site in 1979.

- To document the experiences of the family of an Iraqi War veteran.

- To document our grandfather's service in the National Guard in 1960.

Each of these examples is specific enough to be workable and flexible enough to cover a variety of questions. This statement can be shared with the veteran at the time of initial contact; it should be kept with interview-related materials as part of the oral history documentation.

Initial Contact with the Narrator

Initial contact with a narrator frequently begins with a letter, which is both a mark of respect and the first step in transparency in the interview process. An interview contact letter introduces the interviewer and the oral history interview process. Communicating first by letter gives the veteran time to think about his answer before being asked to make a decision. A telephone call following up the letter then provides an opportunity for the veteran to ask questions about the interview and to discuss his answer. See Appendix D for an example of an interview contact letter.

Following the initial contact, if the veteran has agreed to be interviewed, the interviewer often sets a pre-interview meeting, either by telephone or in person, between interviewer and veteran. This begins interview preparations. During this meeting, guided by a form such as the biographical data form in Appendix C, the interviewer can ask for background about the narrator's time in the Service. This is the time to collect data, not to hear stories. Background information about the narrator's branch of the Service and assignments, types of training programs, peacetime assignments and postings, and post-service career can save time when doing research about topics to discuss in the interview. Interviewers will want to remember, however, that narrators may not be able to provide full details about some experiences; places and place names, for example, can be confused and battle names can change over time. But this preparation, on the whole, can be very helpful for both the narrator and the interviewer. For an interviewer, it provides a starting point for background research for the interview, reveals what is important to the veteran, and begins to suggest ways in which to best frame questions. For a veteran, these preparations can begin their process of thinking about memories that can come up in an interview.

Research

Using the information on the biographical data form as a guide, the interviewer can conduct background research. Research helps prepare the interviewer for the interview by identifying background about the veteran's experiences. It is a critical step and one that all interviewers, even seasoned interviewers and veterans with backgrounds to the veterans, should take, if possible. It can help identify events to mention to the narrator and can pin down details like dates and places that can serve as helpful reminders in an interview. Information for research can be found in public libraries, state and local historian societies, college and university libraries, veterans' museums, and on various websites.

The Veterans History Project Database (http://www.loc.gov/vets/) provides a good example of a source of information about veterans. Information, including interviews, written memoirs, and other materials such as photographs and letters on the database is keyword searchable. It provides background about the types of experience someone may have had and, even if not specific to the narrator, can help suggest topics or questions to include during an interview. A review of the database materials also can suggest gaps in information such as the roles of women or members of ethnic groups that the narrator may be able to fill in.

Other useful information sources include the following:

Newspapers. They contain information from the period during which the veteran served including details about local, state, and national news items. Some may include mention of the narrator, the narrator's family, and/or of other people the narrator may have known—information that can be used to formulate questions that can spur memories.

Letters or diaries. Even if letters or diaries are not from the narrator, if they are from someone who served at the same general time and place, they may include details that will be similar to the veteran's experiences; if so, they can be used to develop questions that can evoke memories.

Maps. Looking at a map of the area in which the veteran served can help orient the interviewer to places that could be discussed during the interview; this can help the interviewer follow the narrator's statements and perhaps bring up ideas for questions.

Photographs. If you uncover photographs of veterans from the places mentioned in the narrator's biographical data form, consider making copies and using them as interview props; be aware the narrator may have also her own photographs to show the interviewer.

Collections in a state historical society, archive, or veterans' museum. These sources may have broad collections of information about veterans' experiences as well as artifacts such as uniforms and medals; many of their collections are digitized and available on the Internet and can be searched for information mentioned in the veteran's biographical data form.

Information from veterans' organizations. These organizations often have people who, like specialists at the museums and archives, can serve as resources for information about veterans' experiences.

Encyclopedias or other standard sources. These sources can provide general background information about the time period of the veteran's service and context for experiences that may be discussed in the interview.

Most of these sources are available locally; the Veterans History Project website and some of the state museum and archives information can be accessed on the Internet. In addition to these sources, Internet searches can turn up other sites that have information about veterans. A word of caution here, however—broad or scattershot Internet research can be overly time-consuming, raise false leads, and include information that has not been reviewed for accuracy. The purpose is to get background about the narrator's experiences that can be used to develop questions and follow-up questions.

Developing an Interview Guide

An interview guide is a list of proposed questions to ask during an interview. It is not a formal list, but a set of questions on themes and topics to help an interviewer guide an interview. Based on the interviewer's background research, the guide usually covers the veteran's experiences, beginning with a short description of the veteran's life before entry into military service and providing some information about the narrator's life after the Service. This broad overview helps put a veteran's service into context, reminding everyone, as Jeff D. Corrigan, Oral Historian at The State Historical Society of Missouri, has said, that even though an interview focuses on the veteran's life in the Service, the life stories of veterans do not end when their service ends.[7]

Developing Interview Themes

Developing an interview guide starts with identifying between three and five content themes to cover in an interview. These themes provide the basic structure for the interview. A set of themes for an interview with a veteran might include the following:

- Entering Military Service

- Daily Life in Military Service

- Assignments in Military Service

- Service in a Combat Zone

- Life after Military Service

- Reflections about Military Service

Interview themes are based on the oral history's statement of purpose and the interviewer's research. Like the statement of purpose, they provide focus for the interview but are broad enough to encourage flexibility in the topics to be covered and the questions to be asked.

Interview themes are then divided into specific topics that an interviewer wants to cover in an interview. After doing the research, a great way to get started is often to brainstorm a wide range of possible interview topics. Following this with thoughtful consideration of the purpose of the interview and the veteran's experiences can help an interviewer develop a manageable set of topics for each theme. Here is an example of the types of topics, organized by themes, that can be used when interviewing veterans:

Developing Interview Topics

Examples of Interview Themes and Topics – General

- Entering Military Service
  - Brief description—life before military service
  - Entering military service and choice of branch of Armed Forces
  - Training

- Daily Life in Military Service
  - Assignments—where and when
  - A day in the life
    - Daily routine
    - Food
    - Clothing
    - Shelter
  - Friendships
  - Recreation and fun (what stands out)
    - Difficulties and hardships (what stands out)
    - Communications with home

- Assignments in the Military Service
  - War zone, non-war zone – describe
  - Purpose of assignment
  - Training/preparation for assignment
    - Weapons issued
  - First memories of assignment
  - Daily life on assignment
    - Food, clothing, shelter
    - Daily responsibilities, expectations

- Routine situations
- Non-routine situations
    - Difficult situations
    - Rest and recuperation (R & R)
    - Communication with home
    - Change of assignment

- Service in a Combat Zone
  - First communication about assignment
  - Purpose of assignment
  - Training for assignment
    - Weapons issued
  - Travel to assignment
  - Living conditions
  - Daily life
    - Daily responsibilities, expectations
    - Friendships
  - Routine situations
  - Non-routine situations
  - Difficult situations
  - R & R
  - Communications with home
  - Completion of assignment

- Life after Military Service
  - Discharge
    - Coming home
    - Reintegrating into family life
    - Re-entry into civilian life
    - Civilian life
        - Marriage/family
        - Education
        - Career
    - Keeping in touch with other veterans
        - VA
        - Reunions
    - Role as a veteran in your community
        - Honor guards
        - Honor flights

- Reflections on Military Service
    - On service
    - On life after service

These examples of themes and topics demonstrate several points that are helpful for interviewers to consider. First, the topics cover not just the veteran's life while in military service but begin with the veteran's life before entering the Service and end with information about the veteran's life after leaving the Service. Second, they follow a basic chronological order, asking about things as they happened during the veteran's service. Putting the topics in this order allows the veteran to move into the rhythm of the interview while providing background and context for the information being conveyed. Third, the assignments discussions are the heart of the interview and thus the list of suggested topics are longest for these themes. Finally, the list of topics ends with reflections. Reflection questions give a veteran the opportunity to put military service and its experiences into perspective and end the interview with the narrator's thoughts and ideas.

This list contains enough topics for an extensive interview. If a veteran is prepared to discuss a number of topics like this, that's fine. But if a veteran doesn't have the stamina to sit through a longer interview, or the inclination to discuss certain topics, it is up to the interviewer to decide which topics to focus on and how to approach the veteran's experience in a respectful, careful way that documents the key aspects of her time in the Service.

This sample list of topics can be used for interviewing veterans in any branch of military service. Based on their research, interviewers can also include topics specific to a particular branch of the Armed Forces or assignment. Each list of topics should be unique and keyed to the individual veteran's experience.

The final interview guide includes a list of questions developed for each chosen theme and topic. Questions in the guide do not need to be numbered or written out in complete sentences but can simply suggest questions or prompts about each theme and topic the interviewer wants to bring up. This is where the interviewer's research really pays off, as it can provide information to decide what to ask and when to ask it.

Developing the Questions

Developing interview questions is an art, as illustrated by the following examples of a couple of the sections in the sample guide developed above.

Entering Military Service (theme)
Talk about your life before entering the Service (introduce the theme)
    Life before service in Armed Forces (topic)
        How you would you describe your life before going into the Service?
            Possible follow-up questions:
                Education?
                Work experience?
Describe your family's military background and traditions
    Possible follow-up questions:
        Military experience of other family members?
        What and when and why or why not?
        Family response to going into the Service?
    Entering and Choice of Branch of Armed Forces (topic)
        Tell me about when and why you entered the Armed Forces
            Possible follow-up question:
                Enlisted or drafted? What's your story?
                Your thoughts about entering the Service and why you did?

        According to the biographical data form, you entered the [insert name of branch of Armed Forces]. Tell me about why you entered this branch of the Armed Forces?
            Possible follow-up questions:
                What about other branches? Why or why not?
                Taking the Oath and then what? Briefly describe your first days in the military

Training (topic)
Basic training—Describe some of your most memorable moments.
    Possible follow-up questions:
        What skills did you learn?
        What did you learn about the military/military life?
        Stories that stand out in your memory

Special training—what was it?
        Why did you receive special training?
        What skills were you taught and why?
            Possible follow-questions:
                Where did you use your training?

Reflections (theme)
Now, as we are ending our interview, let's reflect a little on your time in the Service. (introduce the theme)
    On Being in the Service (topic)
        What did your time in the Service mean to you and why?
        What did you think when you were discharged?

What do you think now?
What are you most proud of and why?
What are you least proud of and why?
Were there turning points for you during your years of service? If so, what were they and what did they mean to you?
If you were asked to comment on the cost of war, what would you want the public to know?

On Life after the Service (topic)
If you were asked to identify the impact of being in the Service on your life, what would you say? Positives? Negatives? Why each?
    How would you describe the readjustment process?
        Impact on you?
        Impact on your family?
Describe your involvement in veteran's organizations and activities.
        When and how and why did you become involved?
        What about Honor Flights.
        What about participation in parades, funerals, and other activities that honor the service of veterans.

These examples of questions illustrate several points for interviewers to consider. The first is that the careful and intentional thought put into the interviews right from the beginning shows in the development of the question guide. There are many questions one can ask a veteran. Decisions on which to ask are based on the purpose and intent of doing the interview. The second point is that the research contributes to development of the question guide by helping identify specific questions that can bring out memories important to the veteran and the veteran's experiences.

Interviews with veterans can cover a broad range of backgrounds and information. Cold War topics can include documenting service at a missile site or construction of missiles and missile sites. Veterans who did not see combat could have been assigned to support services in war zones—a potential theme for an interview. Others will have had experiences such as playing in a military band, being assigned to an occupation force, serving in the United States or abroad during peacetime, or participating in a specialized training program for a specific branch of the Armed Forces. Interviews with women veterans can include questions about being granted permanent status in the Armed Forces after World War II, having opportunities to serve as officers, and lifting the ban on women serving in combat roles. Interviewers can ask narrators of all backgrounds to discuss the end of racial segregation in the Armed Forces in1948 and the integrated military today. Questions about "Don't Ask, Don't Tell" also can be asked of many veterans, including those identifying as LGBTQ (lesbian, gay, bisexual, transgender, queer). Interviews with Native American veterans might include experiences and information related to tribal cultural practices concerning veterans. Question guides can also focus specifically on a branch of the Armed Forces. For example, United States Air Force veterans can be asked about training flights, the planes they flew, the crews they served with, and the specifics of flight assignments. Veterans of the United States Navy can be asked about shipboard training, the shipmates they served with, descriptions of their ships, the places they went and why, and information about the ship's assignments.

Oral historians ask open-ended questions—questions that cannot be answered with a simple "yes" or "no but invite long, thoughtful answers. Questions also should be neutral and not lead the narrator's answers in any one direction. Neutral questions give narrators the opportunity to speak about first-person memories as they see fit.

Like the themes and topics, the questions on an interview guide are typically organized in chronological order. This is the way many people think and the way many memories work. Listing questions as shown in the example—starting with the earliest memories related to the purpose of an interview and working through to the most recent—allows the interviewer to keep the interview moving along in a direction that can be comfortable and encouraging for the narrator.

The sensitivity with which the interviewer asks the questions also helps build rapport and trust between narrator and interviewer. Sorting through and discussing daily life memories before asking experience or combat questions protects the veteran from having to answer difficult questions the minute that the recorder is turned on.

Interviewers want to end an interview on a reflective note whenever possible. Ending with reflections questions, as in the example here, gives the veteran a chance to put his military service into personal perspective and to speak for himself about the meanings of those memories. Regardless of whether the memories are positive or negative, talking about what they mean can be one of the most important parts of the interview for a veteran.

Oral history interviews provide an opportunity for open and candid discussions about the interview themes and topics. There are times when a veteran, working with the interviewer, will identify topics that are off-limits, such as discussion of classified information; these boundaries must be respected. But for the topics that are covered, an interview is a time for a veteran to explore the depth and meaning of memories of military service. See Appendix F for an example of a full interview guide.

Scheduling an Interview

As discussed earlier, the first contact with a narrator before the interview usually is made in writing. After the narrator agrees to do an interview and the interviewer has begun the background research, the interviewer and narrator will want to set a time and place for the interview. When confirming the interview, the interviewer will want to also send along additional information about what will take place. Oral historians often include the following information with the interview confirmation: a reminder about the type of recording equipment (audio, video, or both) that will be used, suggestions about what to wear if the interview will be videotaped, a short list of what to expect during the interview, interviewer contact information (email address and telephone number), and a list of likely interview themes and topics.

Generally, to preserve flexibility in the interview, the interviewer does not send the narrator the specific questions on the question guide. Sending just the themes and topics gives the veteran enough information to mentally prepare for an interview and the flexibility during the interview to talk about the memories in a way that make sense of the past for the narrator. The interviewer then can use the specific questions to guide the interview.

Schedule the interview at a time that is good and at a place that is convenient for the narrator. This is especially true for older narrators, who may not want to schedule more than one thing each day. If the interview is the only thing on the narrator's schedule for the day, this can cut down on distractions that may otherwise affect the quality of his or her participation.

The interviewer will want to assemble an oral history kit and to check it before each interview. An oral history kit often includes the following:

Oral History Interview Recording Kit

- Recorder

- External microphone and cable

- AC adapter and cord or batteries

- Equipment accessories such as microphone stand, video recorder tripod, and headphones

- Extension cords

- Extra recording media

- Two copies of the legal release agreement—one for the narrator and one for the repository, a copy of the interview guide, and the narrator's contact information

- Bottles of water—at least two, one for narrator and one for interviewer

- Snack such as granola bar for narrator to offer if needed during a break

- Tablet such as steno pad for taking notes

- Pen and pencil

- Sign for door saying "oral history interview in progress"

- Recorder manual

- Small camera

- Box of tissues

- Cough drops or mints

Each step before the interview helps prepare the interviewer and the narrator for the interview itself.

1. Stephanie George, Archivist, Center for Oral and Public History (COHP), California State University-Fullerton (CSUF), El Toro Marine Corps Air Station Oral History Project, reply to Questionnaire for Community Oral History Projects, March 2009, as quoted in Mary Kay Quinlan with Nancy MacKay and Barbara W. Sommer, *Community Oral History Toolkit*, vol. 4, *Interviewing in Community Oral History* (Walnut Creek, CA: Left Coast Press, 2013), 23. The El Toro Marine Corps Air Station Oral History Project is a collaboration between Orange County Great Park and the COPH) at CUSF, developed under the direction of COHP Director, Dr. Natalie Fousekis.

2. Sharon Raynor, email to Barbara Sommer, June 15, 2015.

3. Catherine Madison, "Our Dangerous Reluctance to Talk Openly about War," *Star Tribune*, June 25, 2015: A-9.

4. Sue VerHoef, telephone conversation with Barbara Sommer, June 5, 2015.

5. The Oral History Association holds a training session at its annual meeting each year and hosts a military history affinity group for those interested in learning more about the work of military historians and oral history. Its website also offers links to regional associations. http://www.oralhistory.org/resources/, accessed August 23, 2015. The Veterans History Project has trainers in each state available to lead workshops. Check the VHP website for information about how to schedule a workshop. http://www.loc.gov/vets/workshopinfo.html, accessed August 23, 2015.

6. Sarah Milligan, telephone conversation with Barbara Sommer, July 8, 2015.

7. Jeff D. Corrigan, telephone conversation with Barbara Sommer, June 8, 2015.

Captain Larry Schwab
  Larry Schwab Collection (AFC/2001/001/23979), Veterans History Project, American Folklife Center,
  Library of Congress

In May of 2015, William D. Adams, Chairman of the National Endowment for the Humanities (NEH), recorded an oral history interview about his experiences serving during the Vietnam War for the Veterans History Project at the Library of Congress. In a later discussion about that experience, he stated that the more we know about what veterans say and feel about themselves, the better off we all will be, because veterans' stories are an essential part of the larger story of our country. Of particular relevance to the topic of this pamphlet is his comment that oral history interviews honor the veterans and their experiences and create a legacy of stories from which we all can learn.[1]

The personal and national importance of veterans' stories makes it particularly important that interviewers keep oral history principles and best practices in mind while conducting interviews with veterans. As discussed earlier, these principles and practices are the cornerstones of the trust and rapport that an interviewer builds with a narrator during the interview.

The Interview

One of the first decisions in planning the actual interview is determining who will be included as the interview participants. The main participants are the narrator and the interviewer, with interviewers working alone in one-on-one situations. At times, however, interviewers use teams. If an interviewer will be working with a team, this information should be shared with the narrator. Some veterans prefer to confine the interview to just the interviewer and the narrator; if so, respect the veteran's wishes.

Interview Roles

There may be times when others—such as members of the veteran's family—ask to sit in on the interview. The decision on whether to allow this is up to the veteran. A narrator, especially one who has been silent about his or her military experiences prior to the interview, may be reluctant to talk with extra people in the room, including family members. If so, respect the person's wishes. The decision on who will be a part of the interview can influence the rapport and trust between interviewer and narrator, and therefore should be considered carefully.

Trust between an interviewer and narrator is a critical factor in an oral history interview. Interviews focus on memories that often are very personal and perhaps have never been talked about before. It is the interviewer's responsibility not just to listen to these memories but to ask questions about them and to probe their meanings. Because this can be an intense experience for a narrator, especially for many veterans, building trust and rapport between the narrator and interviewer is an important part of the interview process.

Interviewer–Narrator Trust

It is the interviewer's responsibility to build the rapport that is the basis of a trust relationship with the veteran. Rapport starts by being completely open about the reasons for doing the interview. It means explaining the intention of the interview, clearly stating what its purpose is and the reasons for it.

In an interview, the trust relationship also is built on showing respect for the veteran's memories as spoken in the interview. The interviewer and narrator are partners in the interview; it takes both to do it. The interviewer's role is to guide the veteran in telling her story within the limits of ethical and legal practices. Interviewers and narrators should discuss the importance of including as much information as possible in the historical record; this is the purpose of doing an oral history interview. Although some questions can be difficult to ask and discuss—such as women's recent experiences in war zone assignments or the experiences of veterans returning home from Vietnam, for example—the answers can add new information and insight about a place, a time, an event, or a person's life story. On the other hand, if an interviewer agrees not to ask about a specific topic during the interview—shooting people, for example—the decision must be respected; springing a question about an out-of-bounds topic during an interview goes against oral history ethics and is likely to damage the narrator's willingness to be open about his experiences.

The Interview Setting The interviewer or interviewing team is responsible for arranging the interview setting. This begins with arriving on time and bringing everything needed to do the interview.

After arriving, greeting everyone, and making any needed introductions, the interviewer and team can begin to organize the interview setting. This includes checking for ambient sound, deciding on where the narrator and the interviewer (and other members of the team) will sit, and setting up the recorders to ensure they pick up the sound and get a clear picture for video.

Interviewers usually begin by checking the interview setting for ambient sound—background noise that may be filtered out by our brains during face-to-face discussions but will be picked up by a recorder. Examples are portable air conditioners, running appliances, ringing telephones, dripping faucets, chiming clocks, radios and televisions playing, background voices, and noisy pets. The interviewer should turn off radios and televisions and telephone ringers (remembering to turn them back on again after the interview) and ask to put pets in another room if their presence is a distraction. Other people in the home or the area should be asked to stay out of the room where the interview is taking place and to avoid making noise that may be picked up on the recording. Provide the narrator with a glass or bottle of water but hold off on coffee, tea, or food when the recorder is running. The goal is to keep the interview area as quiet as possible; taping an "oral history interview in progress" sign to the door helps, too.

The interviewer and narrator should be able to look directly at one another and hear one another clearly. Other members of an interview team should be seated where they can carry out their responsibilities without disrupting communication between narrator and interviewer.

If the interview is video recorded, the camera should be placed on a tripod to the interviewer's side so that the narrator can face the camera while talking to the interviewer. The narrator's chair should be placed in good light, but not in front of a window or anyplace where the person will be backlit. Video cameras often work well with no extra lighting, but if lights are used, follow the guidelines in "The Art of Lighting for Recording Video Oral History Interviews" on the *Oral History in the Digital Age* website (http://ohda.matrix.msu.edu/2012/06/the-art-of-lighting-for-recording-video/).[2]

If recording in video, the camera should be positioned for a head-and-shoulders shot with enough space over the narrator's head to keep the picture from looking cropped. The shot should allow room for the narrator to shift in the chair without moving out of the frame. Check that the background doesn't contain any unnecessary visual distractions.

Finally, after the equipment is in place, the interviewer should review the legal release agreement and answer any final questions about it before the interview begins. This is a good time to remind the narrator of the need to sign it right after the interview.

Oral historians often think of interviews as having three somewhat distinct parts. Interviews begin with an introduction, move to a discussion of its themes and topics, and end with the narrator's reflections on the memories shared during that discussion.

The Parts of an Oral History Interview

The purpose of the interview introduction is to identify the interview participants and why the interview is being done. Interview Introductions usually contain the following information:

Interview Introduction

- A short statement by the interviewer about the purpose and intent of the interview as understood by the interviewer and narrator. This statement is short, usually less than two minutes in length.

- Identification of the interview participants. This statement includes the full names of the narrator, the interviewer (and interview team if appropriate), the purpose for doing the interview, and the place and date of the interview, as is shown in this example:

> This interview is recorded for the Veterans History Project with [name of narrator], a former [or current] member of [insert branch of Armed Forces]. The interviewer is [name of interviewer] and the other members of the interviewing team are [insert names and roles]. The interview is being recorded at [insert location] on [insert date].

This introduction is the formal beginning of the interview.

The Body of the Interview

In the body of the interview, the interviewer and narrator discuss the interview themes and topics. The interviewer asks questions and gives the narrator time to answer as thoroughly as he wants.

Narrators and interviewers often cover the interview themes and topics in the order they are included on the question guide. For an interview with a veteran, interviewers usually begin by asking a few questions about her background. These questions set the tone of the interview, help break the ice. They also give the interviewer insight into the narrator's communication style. Interviewers then move to questions about the main topic of the interview, which for veterans are their memories of their military service.

Interviewers will want to keep the intent and purpose of the interview in mind when asking questions. They'll also want to keep an eye on the time to make sure they cover key topics in the agreed-upon interview time period. Questions about the themes and topics are where the interviewer probes the narrator's memory in more depth. These questions encourage the narrator to remember events in as much detail as possible and to discuss them openly with the interviewer. This is the part of an interview that may elicit a later comment from a narrator about not realizing she could "remember so much." These questions also can bring up difficult memories in detail, a situation an interviewer will want to be sensitive to. Discussions of difficult memories can provide information of the depth that oral historians seek in an interview, but they can be very hard for both narrator and interviewer to cover. Based on an understanding of the importance of the contributions these memories can make to the historical record, decisions on how to handle them should be made jointly by the interviewer and narrator.

Oral history interviews usually end with questions that encourage the narrator to reflect on the meanings of her memories. These questions can help the veteran make sense of the past with depth that can add immeasurably to the interview. Usually this involves several open-ended questions about the narrator's thoughts. Asking a narrator about his or her thoughts at the time of discharge and his or her thoughts now could bring out additional insights.

Oral history interviewing guidelines are based on research, preparation, good listening skills—and the Oral History Association *Principles and Best Practices*. When conducting an interview, interviewers are advised to review the *Principles and Best Practices* and to especially remember the following points:

Respect the narrator's story. Asking a narrator to talk about his memories is asking for a gift of information. Showing respect for the narrator's story honors the narrator.

An oral history interview is not a conversation. Conversations are give-and-take discussions. Interviews, on the other hand, are directed question-and-answer sessions in which the interviewer asks open-ended questions and listens while the narrator answers them.

Remember the purpose and intent of the interview. Interviews can be done for many reasons and can cover many different parts of a narrator's life. Remaining focused on the purpose of an interview and the particular themes and topics listed in the question guide helps move it along and keep it centered. Keeping this purpose in mind also helps the narrator by encouraging him or her to concentrate on the specific memories to be covered in the interview.

Be clear about the interviewer's and narrator's roles in the interview. The roles of interviewers and narrators both are important in an interview. Oral history interviews are co-created documents; they are the result of an interaction between narrator and interview in the interview setting. A clear understanding of each person's roles and contributions is basic to oral history ethics and helps guide the interaction in the interview.

Be sensitive to the narrator's unique situation. Narrators may be aged, frail, or nervous, Some may become emotional when talking about certain memories. Use common sense and be prepared to respond to a narrator's needs. Keeping this in mind is an oral history ethical best practice.

Interviewing Tips   While conducting an interview, follow these tips:

Ask open-ended questions. Open-ended questions frequently begin with "Tell me why…" "Tell me about….," or "Describe the….". Questions, prompts, and follow-up questions that begin with *who, what, why, where, when,* and *how* also often result in longer and more detailed answers. The following are examples of closed-ended and open-ended questions and prompts:

Closed-ended:
Did you enlist?
Did you serve overseas?

Open-ended:
Tell me about entering military service. What were the circumstances for you?
Why did you enter the [branch of the Armed Forces]?
Describe hearing about your first deployment. How did it come about for you?

Ask neutral questions. People bring their own personal values, attitudes, biases, and cultural assumptions to an interview. Realizing and recognizing this, try to ask questions in as neutral a way as possible. Neutral questions encourage the narrator to answer openly and give a full account of the information. Leading questions, on the other hand, send a limiting message about the type of answer that is expected, as they can appear to indicate that the interviewer expects a specific answer. Examples of leading and neutral questions are the following:

Leading question:
You must have been pretty upset when you received orders for your first deployment. How did that feel?

Neutral question:
Tell me about receiving orders for your first deployment. What were the circumstances for you?

Listen carefully. Oral history interviewers are careful and attentive listeners. This is a skill that shows respect for the narrator's information and builds trust and rapport in an interview. Interviews often have what oral historian Linda Shopes describes as a measured, thinking-out-loud quality,[3] the result of perceptive and observant listening.

Draw on background research. Background research, in addition to serving as a resource for developing the question guide, provides the interviewer with context for the interview. Use the background research to help clarify a narrator's responses with follow-up questions and to make decisions—often on the spot—about how to handle unexpected information if it comes up. Examples of follow-up questions are the following:

Follow-up question:
You gave an excellent description of life in the camp, but I wonder how the Army managed to get everyone fed three times a day. KP was a big part of many veterans' lives. What do you remember most about your experiences with KP?

Follow-up question:
You mentioned the importance of the friends you made in the Service. What about some of the fun times you had with them? Tell me about a couple of memorable times.

Try to establish the narrator's connection to the information. Oral history narrators have first-person knowledge about events discussed in an interview. During the interview, ask questions that help determine the narrator's connections to its themes and topics. Examples of questions that establish a narrator's connection to the information are the following:

Question examples:
Where were you when all of this happened?
What do you remember most about that day?

Respect stated boundaries. Before an interview, a narrator and an interviewer may identify certain topics that will not be covered in the interview. For example, in an interview with a veteran, the narrator may state that some of her information is classified and cannot be discussed. These boundaries must be respected. Not doing so can destroy rapport and trust between interviewer and narrator and may result in the loss of the interview.

Don't balk at asking questions about controversial or difficult topics. Oral history interviewers, while respecting agreed-on boundaries, do not shy away from asking questions about controversial or difficult topics. Questions about difficult topics often get at memories that have the most meaning for a narrator. Controversial or difficult topics must be handled with care and asked about with neutral, open-ended questions, but they can be some of the most fruitful or meaningful of an interview.

Ask one question at a time. Run-on questions that cover a number of subjects are confusing to both interviewer and narrator. Questions that focus on a single point are easier for the narrator to answer. Examples of run-on and focused questions are the following:

Run-on question:
Tell me about enlisting. What was it like to leave home? How did your family feel? What about your physical? Did you like military food? Where did you sleep? What clothes were you issued? Did they fit?

Focused question:
Tell me about enlisting; why did you make this decision?

Although each of the questions in the run-on question are good ones, they shouldn't be asked all at once. The focused question can be followed up with the other questions.

Don't interrupt. Good listening skills include not interrupting. This holds true even if the narrator is telling a story that appears rehearsed. If this happens, listen to the entire story and take notes about points to cover with follow-up questions, but do not break in or interrupt the story. Wait until the narrator finishes to ask those questions.

Don't challenge a narrator's information. Interviewers may hear information in an interview that they do not agree with or that they may know or suspect is incorrect. Rather than challenging a narrator's information, the interviewer should draw on project research to ask neutral, open-ended questions about why the narrator is saying this and what it means to him. The answers could open up new areas of inquiry and lead to new insights about the topics being discussed as well as the narrator's understanding of a particular time period and events. The difference between challenging and probing questions can be seen in the following examples:

Challenging question:
I was there and that is not how it happened. Everybody knows that. Where were you anyway?

Probing question:
What you have said is new information to me; newspaper articles about this event present it differently. Help me understand your information and point of view. Why do you remember it this way?

Use body language, not verbal comments, to provide positive feedback to the narrator. Interviews involve at least two people—an interviewer and a narrator. The interviewer's role as an active listener includes encouraging the narrator to answer questions in as much detail as possible. Vocal or verbal interruptions, however, that are common in general conversation—such as *uh-huh, yep, I understand*—are intrusive and interrupt the speaker and the narrative in an oral history interview. Interviewers use body language instead. Maintaining eye contact, nodding the head, leaning forward in the chair, and smiling all are non-verbal positive messages that encourage the narrator to continue with an answer. A slight furrowing of the brow can encourage the narrator to expand on or clarify a point. A time-out sign can signal a break. Silent methods of communication maintain contact between interviewer and narrator while preserving good sound quality in the interview.

Respect silence. In general conversation, people often feel the need to fill silence with more conversation. But in oral history interviews, silence is often an essential part of the narrator's thought process and pattern of communication. Silence may mean the narrator is thinking about how to answer a question or make a specific point, or it may mean the narrator is working to control his emotions. Whatever the reason, giving the narrator space to think and respond is part of the oral history interview process, even if it feels unnatural to you. And don't assume silence means the narrator has finished answering a question. It may be that she is just getting started.

Watch for emotions. Oral history interviews can be intense. They involve asking what can be described as personal questions about topics that narrators may not have talked about before. Talking about memories in depth can bring up details in the narrator's mind that make a good oral history, but talking about memories can bring back the emotions that accompanied them, too. If a narrator appears to become emotional during an interview, the interviewer should give the narrator time to compose himself and then focus on asking questions that give him an opportunity to reflect on those memories.

Read body language. Narrators communicate information about their memories through verbal and non-verbal messages. Non-verbal communications are transmitted through body language, such as breaking eye contact, crossing arms, touching the face or neck, grimacing, becoming restless, and rubbing the hands or legs. Narrators also may react by not answering a question or withdrawing emotionally from an interview. Interviewers seeing these signs can put the recorder on pause and ask the narrator if she is doing all right or if it is time for a break. Using non-verbal communication—smiling, nodding, leaning forward—also can help a narrator realize that the interviewer empathizes with his position.

Listen for voice cues. Voice cues are another way that a narrator communicates during an interview. Vocal tone and pitch provide non-verbal messages. These can include pitch and volume changes, inflections, sighs, a wavering or breaking voice, speaking at a different pace, and changing tone, such as in the use of sarcasm. These cues can be handled the same way as body language cues.

Be sensitive to appearance. The narrator's appearance provides another non-verbal clue for the interviewer during an interview. A veteran coming to an interview in uniform sends a powerful message about the importance of serving in the Armed Forces. Acknowledging this helps build rapport between interviewer and narrator. Recognize this, make a note of it, and discuss it with the narrator.

Pace the interview. Interviews tend to develop rhythms. The interviewer and narrator learn to read one another's responses as they work their way through the interview themes and topics. As the interview progresses, it is up to the interviewer to introduce the critical themes and topics in a timely and organized fashion.

Use photos, maps, and other archival materials and artifacts to help jog memories. Visual cues can often prompt narrators' memories. Photographs and maps are good examples, as are newsletters and letters. Questions about uniforms and medals also can open up areas of discussion. When visual prompts are used, interviewers introduce questions about them by describing them in detail for the record. With the narrator's permission, copies of visual materials, labelled to correspond to questions about them, can be kept with the interview materials.

Take notes. Interviewers often jot down notes during the interview about questions and possible follow-up questions to use. The note-taker, whether a separate team member or the interviewer, also writes down place and proper names mentioned in the interview for use in checking spelling and acronyms or jargon mentioned to clarify them with the narrator during or after the interview.

Keep track of time and take breaks. Oral history interviews often last no longer than 90 minutes. It is difficult for people to sit and listen or talk longer than that. Taking a break partway through gives everyone a chance to get up and move around, use the bathroom, have a snack, or take a cigarette break. The interviewer and narrator also can use the break time to assess where they are in the interview and what they still want to cover.

As the interview begins to come to an end, the interviewer should ask the narrator if there is anything important has been missed or overlooked. This gives the narrator a chance to add information that may have been forgotten or not addressed.

An interviewer who has thought carefully about the interview beforehand can use the interview guide to make sure that the critical topics and questions are covered, regardless of the general order of the discussion. As narrators begin to talk about their memories, the actual order of topics discussed in the interview may differ from that in the question guide. This is okay. The guide identifies topics and questions to be covered; the order in which they are covered is the result of the interaction between narrator and interviewer. The guide and the background research used to help prepare it also are useful if the interviewer needs to make decisions about how to handle unexpected information from the narrator.

Interviewers should practice being good listeners. Listening in an oral history interview is an art. An interview is not a dialogue, a conversation, an argument, or an equal exchange of information. An interview is a question-and-answer session in which the interviewer asks the questions and then listens carefully and respectfully to the narrator's answers. Even if the interviewer and narrator share many of the same experiences, it is the interviewer's responsibility to serve as an attentive and respectful listener.

Interviews are dynamic. Although most interviews go quite smoothly, interviewers will want to be prepared for any of the following situations that may emerge.

What If?

Narrators want to repeat information that is general knowledge. Interviews should focus on a narrator's unique memories. If a narrator seems caught up in providing information that is readily available elsewhere, ask questions that focus on the narrator's specific knowledge. The interviewer also may want to ask the narrator what she thinks about the general information she has mentioned.

Narrators forget a name or a date. Don't let the lack of a name or a date interrupt the narrative. Reassure the narrator that specific names and dates can be filled in on the notes after the interview. If you can quickly locate the information based on your research notes, do so. The interviewer also can ask the narrator to provide just a general description of the person or the time period in question—"my captain" or "a few months later," for instance. Remember that even if narrators are sometimes confused about certain details, their memories of experiences and the insights about they bring to a narrative usually remain strong and clear.

Narrators appear to go off the subject. Here interviewers can draw on their background readings and notes to help determine whether the information is new and pertinent or is truly off the subject. If warranted, the interviewer can ask the narrator to provide more information about her connection to the new information. To get the interview back on track, the interviewer can ask a question from the interview guide.

Narrators anticipate the interviewer's questions and answer them in one long statement. Narrators often begin to anticipate questions in an interview, but if the interview starts to turn into a long monologue, one option is to let him continue and take notes about information to clarify after the narrator has finished speaking. Although interviewers do not as a general rule interrupt narrators, the interviewer also can draw on background research and a sense of how the narrator responds to questions to decide if—or when—a question is warranted in this situation.

Narrators ask for a response from the interviewer. Asking questions such as "What do you think?" of one's listeners is a polite and standard conversational response. But because interviews are not conversations, the appropriate response is to remind the narrator that the purpose of the interview is to record the narrator's information and thoughts.

Narrators make negative comments about other people. Listen carefully for comments that might constitute slander (a false or damaging statement about a person) and be sensitive to the possible effects of defamation (damaging a person's reputation). Consider asking the narrator, "Are you sure you want to continue?" If you are worried about the interpersonal or legal ramifications of a narrator's comments about others, consult John A. Neuenschwander's *A Guide to Oral History and the Law*, 2nd edition. Review the information and examples in the book and use them as a guide to help make decisions about how to handle the situation.[4] If needed, consult a local legal expert. Also consider restricting access to the interview for a specified period of time.

Narrators bring out photographs, uniforms, medals, or other memorabilia during an interview. Review the materials with the narrator, describing each in detail for the record, and use them as visual cues during the interview. If the narrator gives permission, include copies with the interview materials. The repository also may be interested in the items. If so, and again with the narrator's consent, use a photograph/memorabilia/artifact form to identify the materials and then follow the directions from the repository on how to handle the items.

Narrators bring up stories after the recorder is turned off. Answering questions about a specific time and place often stimulates narrators to remember details they had not thought about for a long time. But sometimes a narrator's recollections don't stop when the recorder is turned off and the stories keep coming. When this happens, the interviewer and narrator can discuss whether to turn the recorder back on or schedule another interview.

Sensitive Issues

Certain sensitive issues that may come up in oral history interviews require extra thought and care. Many of the following are common to the oral history interviewing process in general, but can be especially important to consider when interviewing veterans.

Aging Narrators

Every day we are losing many of our remaining World War II veterans, and Korean and many Vietnam War veterans are now also senior citizens. Here are several tips on working with aging narrators. As with all oral history interview guidelines, they are based on best practices, ethics, respect for the narrator, and a certain amount of common sense.

- Be sensitive to the narrator's daily schedule. As noted earlier, older people often find it tiring or distracting to schedule more than one activity a day. An interview takes time and energy. Try to schedule it on a day when the narrator has nothing else planned.

- Schedule the interview at an accessible location. Often interviews take place in a person's home or a familiar location. Be sure when scheduling the interview that the location is readily accessible to the veteran. If at a location other than the veteran's home, make sure entrances are accessible and parking is available.

- Communicate information about the interview to the veteran and the veteran's caregivers beforehand and at the beginning of the interview. Let everyone know what the interview involves, why it is being done, and when and where it will be conducted. Check on the need to have a caregiver present, but stress that the interview is an opportunity for the veteran to tell his story.

- Remember that as people age, their long-term memories, especially of eventful or traumatic situations, often remain more vivid than their short-term memories. The veteran may not be able to remember an event from a week ago but can clearly recount difficult experiences from several decades past.

- Older veterans may share stories that they've told many times and that accordingly have taken on a rehearsed quality. If this should happen, don't interrupt the story to ask a question; the narrator may find this confusing and it could affect the rapport between interviewer and narrator. Let the veteran tell the story and ask follow-up questions after the story has been told. Also be prepared to understand that the story may be all that the veteran can recall about the experience, as telling and re-telling a story can cement that version in the veteran's memory and other specific details may have been lost in the process.

- Physical factors also may be an issue. Older people can be physically frail and lack stamina. Older veterans also may have health issues that are aggravated by age. Sensitivity to this situation during the interview may mean taking additional breaks, providing the veteran with a snack during a break (such as a granola bar from the Oral History Interview Kit), or just putting the recorder on pause to sit quietly for a while so the veteran can gather energy to continue the interview.

- Other physical conditions can affect narrator–interviewer communication. If the veteran cannot hear well or cannot see the interviewer, set up the interview accordingly. The interviewer may have to sit close to the veteran to be heard, speak more loudly than normal, and repeat questions several times. Such situations usually do not affect the narrator's memory, but they should be handled with sensitivity and respect.

- The interview may serve as an end-of-life interview for the narrator. This is an ethical issue and a responsibility not to be taken lightly. Veterans often become more willing to talk about their experiences as they get older, but if a veteran chooses to break her silence about her time in military service as she nears the end of her life because of illness, for example, the interview is likely to have a profound meaning for her. In such a case, questions and the veteran's responses should be handled with the utmost respect and care.

- Families may want to hear the veteran's story. This situation comes up often with aging veterans, as families often want to make sure a veteran tells his story while he still is able to do so. While families may have the best of intentions, in reality family members may not be prepared to hear or understand a veteran's full story. As has been noted previously, the decision on whether to talk about time in military service is the veteran's alone and must be respected.

- Aging veterans may have undiagnosed Post-Traumatic Stress Disorder (PTSD). Diagnoses of PTSD among veterans of earlier conflicts are not as common as they have become now, but that does not mean that older veterans aren't affected by it. Indeed, some veterans are being diagnosed at the age of 80 and older. See below for some suggested guidelines on handling PTSD.

- Aging veterans may lack adequate help and support. If an interviewer finds that a veteran is living in a vulnerable or threatening situation, it is strongly recommended that the interviewer not become directly involved, but instead report the situation to proper authorities.

- Aging veterans may speak more openly than expected. If a veteran says things that appear to be out of character or inappropriate, try to guide him or her to a more appropriate topic or approach. If this can't be done, the interviewer should consider ending the interview and document the reason for doing this.

- Informed consent is another ethical issue that interviewers should be sensitive to. If an older veteran seems unable to understand the purpose of the interview, or where the interview will be deposited, he either should not be interviewed or should be interviewed only in the most carefully controlled and ethical circumstances possible.

- Be prepared. Interviewers always should be prepared for unusual or unexpected circumstances when doing an interview. This is especially important when working with an aging veteran. Watch for signs that indicate the veteran may need a break or may not be comfortable with a line of questioning and respond respectfully and compassionately.

A practical and ethical issue that is of particular relevance to conducting interviews with veterans is Post-Traumatic Stress Disorder (PTSD), a mental health condition that is typically caused by exposure to a difficult or terrifying event. Although veterans of all wars may struggle with similar symptoms, the long wars in Afghanistan and Iraq have

Post-Traumatic Stress Disorder (PTSD)

brought this condition to the attention of the American public. According to the United States Department of Veterans Affairs, PTSD afflicts approximately:

- 30 percent of Vietnam veterans

- 10 percent of Gulf War (Desert Storm) veterans

- 11 percent of veterans of the war in Afghanistan

- 20 percent of Iraqi war veterans[5]

It is estimated that these statistics will most probably increase over time. Veterans also may experience late onset stress symptoms (LOSS), which can be similar to PTSD.[6]

Speaking about some events or situations can trigger symptoms of PTSD. The information included here should not take the place of any kind of medical or professional help. According to the editors of *Listening on the Edge: Oral History in the Aftermath of Crisis*,[7] interviewers should watch for the following types of indicators when conducting an oral history interview with a veteran who may have traumatic memories that can trigger PTSD:

- Difficulty concentrating, fidgeting, shaking or quivering hands, breaking eye contact, repetitive hand gestures, change in breathing patterns, or emotional volatility.

- Indications that the veteran is experiencing sights, sounds, smells, and feelings of the memories when describing them.

- Emotions and tears.

- Telling memories in a less-than-coherent fashion, with specifics about time and place needing to be filled in later.

Interviewers should familiarize themselves with these tips and use them to help monitor an interview. If an interviewer knows the veteran has been diagnosed with PTSD or observes signs of PTSD, be guided by the following:

- When setting up the interview, encourage the veteran to choose a place to sit that feels safe and comfortable.

- Use warm, open facial features and eye contact to maintain a connection with the veteran during the interview. Leaning forward and dipping the chin can be more effective in encouraging the veteran to continue a story than nodding when the veteran is discussing traumatic memories.

- If the veteran becomes emotional, put the recorder on pause and give him time to deal with the emotions. Emotions can be cathartic. Don't anticipate them but bring out the tissues if needed. Don't touch the veteran; let her work through the emotions on her own. If at all possible, try to continue the interview and end with reflection questions.

- Realize that talking about a traumatic memory can, in some cases, validate or help a veteran make sense of an experience; veterans sometime indicate a readiness to talk about traumatic memories that can help an interviewer decide whether to continue with the discussion.

- Respect the veteran's use of silence and watch for signs that she is ready to continue; silence can be a powerful part of the veteran's pattern of communication about traumatic memories.

- Give the veteran time and psychological space to process the memories during the interview; don't rush or push him in any way.

- Handle confessional memories with sensitivity, but remember that an interview is not a counseling session and interviewers are not healers. Try to redirect if the interview seems to be getting off track. If a veteran mentions involvement in something that may be illegal, stop the interview and seek legal advice as soon as possible.

- Try not to over-react or over-identify with the veteran during the interview or to shut down emotionally. It may help narrator and interviewer for the interviewer to ask the narrator how she coped with the situation at the time and how she copes with it now.

- As a precaution, keep a phone number of a contact person for the veteran handy in case the veteran needs help.

As was stated by Cynthia Macauley, a counselor at the Duluth, Minnesota, Veterans Administration Center, at a workshop for volunteer interviewers hosted by the St. Louis County Historical Society Veterans Memorial Hall, the interviewer's role is not to understand a veteran's experience, but to help the veteran tell his or her story.[8]

The Cost of War

One of the purposes for doing interviews with veterans is to document the human perspective of their experiences. Interviews with veterans who have served in wartime inevitably involve discussions about the cost of war, never an easy task. Yet most veterans agree with oral historian and U.S. Army Cold War veteran Paul Ortiz about the importance of having and sharing those discussions. As he wrote recently, "We, as veterans, are simply asking the civilians who send people off to war to remember that they can never, during their own lifetimes, declare that war to have ended. In other words, there is never a 'mission accomplished' point in a war; that's a myth. Documenting the 'cost of war' allows us to commemorate our fallen comrades in a unifying manner regardless of political viewpoints. You can be anti-war [or] pro-war.... The most important aspect...is to have a space where we can remember our fallen comrades with honor. This is what we mean by the 'cost of war.'"[9] U.S. Army Specialist and Afghan War veteran Brock Robert McIntosh also emphasized this perspective in his Veterans History Project interview: "It's always the means that justify the ends. ... The thing is, there's never a war that ends war."[10]

Oral histories with veterans allow us to listen to their voices and experiences as we consider how to assess and reckon with the cost of war. Questions about the meaning of the cost of war to the veteran or of how he remembers and honors friends can help document this information. As combat chaplain David W. Peters has written, "Oral historians remind society how big decisions, made by powerful leaders, affect ordinary people."[11]

At the End of the Interview

At the end of an oral history interview, the interviewer should first thank the narrator, and both the narrator and interviewer then should sign the legal release agreement clarifying copyright status of the interview and identifying responsibility for its ongoing preservation, access, and use. The next step is to take a picture of the veteran in the interview setting, even if the interview was video-recorded; this provides visual documentation of the interview for the repository. A copy of the photograph also can be included in an interview transcript or index. After finishing these tasks, it is time to pack up the recording equipment, review when the veteran will hear from the interviewer about receiving a copy of the interview, and say good-bye.

With this, the interviewer's responsibility for doing the interview comes to an end, but responsibility for the oral history does not. The after-interview steps described in the next section of this pamphlet help guide the interviewer through the rest of the oral history process.

References

1. "NEH Chairman William Adams on the Veterans History Project," www.youtube.com/watch?v=D91LnT3DHMw, accessed June 10, 2015.

2. Douglas A. Boyd, "The Art of Lighting for Recording Video Oral History Interviews," in *Oral History in the Digital Age*, edited by Douglas A. Boyd, Steve Cohen, Brad Rakerd, and Dean Rehberger. Washington, D.C.: Institute of Museum and Library Services, 2012, http://ohda.matrix.msu.edu/2012/06/the-art-of-lighting-for-recording-video/, accessed 7/13/2015.

3. Linda Shopes, "What Is Oral History?" History Matters: The U.S. Survey Course on the Web, http://historymatters.gmu.edu/mse/oral/what.html, accessed Aug 30, 2015.

4. John A. Neuenschwander, *A Guide to Oral History and the Law, 2nd ed.* (New York, NY: Oxford University Press, 2014).

5. *NIH Medline Plus*, http://www.nlm.nih.gov/medlineplus/magazine/issues/winter09/articles/winter09pg10-14.html, accessed August 7, 2015.

6. *PTSD: National Center for PTSD*, United States Department of Veterans Affairs, http://www.ptsd.va.gov/public/types/war/ptsd-older-vets.asp, accessed August 7, 2015.

7. These tips are from Mark Cave, "Introduction: What Remains, Reflections on Crisis Oral History," and Stephen M. Sloan, "Conclusion: The Fabric of Crisis, Approaching the Heart of Oral History," Mark Cave and Stephen M. Sloan, eds., *Listening on the Edge: Oral History in the Aftermath of Crisis* (New York: Oxford University Press, 2014). 1-14, 262-274. Additional information was provided by oral historian Troy Reeves in a telephone conversation with Barbara Sommer, June 19, 2015, and by Cynthia Macaulay of the Duluth Veterans Administration Center at a Veterans Memorial Hall Oral History Program workshop at the St. Louis County Historical Society, Duluth, MN, August 6, 2015. For a discussion about the impact of PTSD on women nurses who served in Vietnam, see Kim Heikkila, *Sisterhood of War: Minnesota Women in Vietnam* (St. Paul, MN: Minnesota Historical Society, 20110, 117-136.

8. Macauley made these comments during the Duluth veterans interviewer training session cited above.

9. Professor Paul Ortiz, U.S. Army veteran, Cold War, email to Clifford Matthew Kuhn, January 22, 2015. Forwarded with permission from Clifford Kuhn to Barbara Sommer, May 11, 2015.

10. Spec. McIntosh was with the United States Army/Army National Guard. He served in Operation Enduring Freedom (OEC). (AFC2001/001/86819), Veterans History Project, American Folklife Center, Library of Congress.

11. David W. Peters, "A Spiritual War: Crises of Faith in Combat Chaplains from Iraq and Afghanistan," in *Listening on the Edge*, 239.

Captain Ann Catherine Cunningham
Ann Catherine Cunningham Collection (AFC/2001/001/48446), Veterans History Project, American Folklife Center, Library of Congress

The interview is done, the legal release form is signed, the equipment is packed up, and the interviewer is heading home. It is now time to move to the after-interview tasks.

After the Interview

When we think of oral history, we think of recorded interviews that will be available to people into the future. This availability of an interview, whole, unedited, and in recorded and, often, print format, is what helps set oral history apart from other types of interviews. But ongoing access to the interviews doesn't just happen. It takes a commitment by an interviewer to see the process through.

A written thank-you note or letter acknowledges the gift of information given by the narrator. It also provides another opportunity to review the after-interview steps with the narrator, such as when it will be submitted to a repository and how it will be handled. And if an additional interview, or more than one interview, is needed, this is a good time to begin making arrangements for the next session. See Appendix D for an example of a thank you letter.

Thank the Veteran

Preservation begins as soon as possible after the interview. The first step is to carefully check the interview recording. Make sure both the narrator's and interviewer's voices, and the voices of any other participants, can clearly be heard and that the interview can be played from beginning to end. Then immediately make several copies. As archivists and others who work with oral histories know, the time right after an interview is a vulnerable period for the recording. Taking care of these steps as quickly as possible helps preserve and protect it. The original copy should be labeled the master recording and stored, unchanged, in the format in which it was recorded. Making a copy of the interview in a compressed, commonly available format to accompany the master copy will help the repository provide broad access to the interview information for users. See the *Oral History in the Digital Age* website for the most up-to-date information about making and keeping copies of interview recordings (http://ohda.matrix.msu.edu/).[1]

Interview Preservation and Access

Interviewers can also enable such access to the recorded interviews by creating indexes and transcripts of the interview content. Indexes identify the topics discussed at particular times in an interview and can be helpful for users who are looking for an overview of the topics or for specific information. They are developed by the interviewer or by an indexer or transcriber working with the interviewer. Transcripts— word-for-word records of the interview—offer a written form of access to the full interview content. If developing a transcript, use a standard format and key the transcript to specific places in the recording. After it is typed, do an audit-edit to check it for accuracy. This is done by listening to the interview while reading the transcript. In both indexes and transcripts, check for accurate spelling of proper and place names. This also is a good time to check for missing or incomplete information that can be further documented on the forms or followed up on in a subsequent interview. And, don't forget to include interview copyright information on both indexes and transcripts.[2]

Repositories also often have certain specifications about producing indexes and transcripts and may have certain recommended styles. Interviewers will want to check with the repository for details about producing indexes and transcripts and follow the directions as provided.

Complete Forms and Notes

Commonly used interview forms are designed to document background and provide context for future users of the interview information. Completing each is another step in the after-interview process; it is sometimes described as creating a paper trail for the interview. Interviewers will want to make sure the narrator's full name is spelled correctly, is stated as the narrator wants it, and is consistent on all forms, as this is how it will appear on all descriptive materials for the interview going forward.

Additional Materials

The after-interview steps for oral history interviews also can include identifying additional materials provided by the narrator, such as photographs, letters, diaries, and memoirs, and artifacts such as uniforms and medals. If the veteran is interested in donating any of these items to a repository, check with the repository and offer to put the veteran in contact with a person there who can help with the donation process. Each repository will have its own guidelines about what it can and cannot accept. The Veterans History Project, for example, can accept original copies of photographs, letters, diaries, and memoirs, but not copies of photographs or artifacts such as uniforms or other materials. It has its own process and forms for submitting materials (http://www.loc.gov/vets/vets-questions.html).

Submission of Materials

The interview process, beginning before the interview and continuing through the interview and these final after-interview steps, comes to an end with the submission of the interview and its related materials to the selected repository. This involves sending all materials—the master recording, a copy of the recording, the signed release form, all completed forms and notes, a transcript or index, and the photograph of the narrator in the interview setting—to the repository. To submit the materials, follow the instructions provided by the repository. Be sure everything is complete and clearly labeled, all names are clearly and correctly spelled, and all recording formats are clearly identified. Deliver the materials in person or follow the mailing instructions from the repository. Include a letter of transmittal, such as the example in Appendix D. And with that—congratulations on completing an oral history interview!

Primary care for oral histories and related materials is provided by a repository such as the Veterans History Project. University libraries and archives, state and local historical societies, and museums also hold collections of interviews with veterans. Repositories catalogue the oral histories, maintain them in climate-controlled conditions, and migrate them to new technologies when needed—and they make them available to users who want to learn from the information they contain

Ongoing Preservation and Access

Advances in technology have expanded options for access to interview information. As oral historian Doug Boyd notes, the combination of digital recording technology and Internet access options is transforming the way we record and convey history. Websites, though not permanent repositories, can provide broad access. When given permission by narrators, many websites include copies of their interview recordings, transcripts, or both, expanding access exponentially. With these postings, one-on-one interviews recorded by interviewers and narrators in relative privacy become available to researchers around the world. This is an exciting and complex area of change and growth in oral history, but it comes with questions, including those focusing on understanding interview content protection and privacy issues. These questions emphasize the importance of following ethical and legal standards and best practices in the careful review of oral histories before posting on a website. For more information about these issues or to find out about the latest technological developments and their impact on oral history, see the *Oral History in the Digital Age* website (http://ohda. matrix.msu.edu/).[3]

Users of oral histories speak and write about the importance of recording and preserving memories spoken in the interviews. Each person's story has embedded in it meanings that are important to the narrator and that help shed light on the time period and events described. This is a fascinating area of scholarship and inquiry; for veterans, it highlights the importance of each person's interview and its contribution to a national and international narrative. There also is another side to the importance of memories for the narrators, however—this is the pride many have of recording their oral histories. Louis Kornhauser, a World War II veteran and contributor to the Veterans History Project, described it as a privilege. As he said, "I'm …here to tell [my] story and it's very meaningful."[4] Oral historian and professor Paul A. Ortiz, a sergeant with the U.S. Army in the 82nd Airborne Division and the 7th Special Forces Group during the Cold War, emphasized the importance of each

The Importance of Memories

individual's voice. As he put it, "Having these interviews allows us to give veterans a voice."[5] These statements remind us of the importance of veterans' information and of the meaning that veterans attach to putting their memories on the record when they are ready to do so.

Uses of the Oral Histories

Users of oral histories with veterans range from scholars of military history to social scientists to family historians to students. The interviews provide information—using just a few examples from the Veterans History Project as examples—about women nurses' perspectives on desegregation during the Korean War, American GIs descriptions of playing Mahjong in the Pacific Theater during World War II, and how the long-term health of American GIs was affected by the hygiene practices they learned during that war. These are truly the human experiences of veterans. Information in the many interviews recorded with veterans held in collections throughout the country is used in publications, exhibitions, secondary and post-secondary education projects, art projects, creative writing projects, website development, and plays and performances. A few examples of these uses are the Project Jukebox Website about Cold War Nike missile sites in Alaska developed by the Digital Branch of the University of Alaska Fairbanks Oral History Program (http://jukebox.uaf.edu/site7/akcoldwar).[6] The Library of Congress has published several books based on Veterans History Project interviews—*Voices of War: Stories of Service from the Home Front and the Front Lines*[7] and *Forever a Soldier: Unforgettable Stories of Wartime Service.*[8] *Freedom Flyers: The Tuskegee Airmen of World War II* is based on oral history interviews done by the National Park Service's Tuskegee Airmen Oral History Project.[9] The experiences of women nurses in Vietnam are examined in *Sisterhood of War: Minnesota Woman in Vietnam.*[10] Exhibitions at museums throughout the country, ranging from the Smithsonian Institutions and the National World War II Museum to state and local historical societies, draw on the first-person recorded memories of veterans to help interpret our history. But above all, oral history interviews with veterans help document their service and make the information available to interested users, whoever they may be. An interviewer's commitment to doing an oral history with a veteran is a gift to the veteran and to this history.

1. See the *Oral History in the Digital Age* website for detailed and up-to-date information. http://ohda.matrix.msu.edu/, accessed August 28, 2015.

2. For more information, check with individual repositories about guidelines for indexes and transcripts. See also the *Style Guide: A Quick References for Editing Oral History Transcripts*, Baylor Institute for Oral History, 2015, http://www.baylor.edu/oralhistory/doc.php/14142.pdf, accessed August 31, 2015. For information on an enhanced Web-based system for access to oral history information, Oral History Metadata Synchronizer (OHMS) at the Louie B. Nunn Center for Oral History, University of Kentucky Libraries, oralhistoryonline.org, accessed August 31, 2015.

3. See also Barbara W. Sommer, *Practicing Oral History in Historical Organizations* (Walnut Creek, CA: Left Coast Press, Inc., 2015).

4. Louis H. Kornhauser (AFC 2001/001/100465), Veterans History Project Collection, American Folklife Center, Library of Congress.

5. Professor Ortiz served in the U.S. Army from 1982-1988 as a paratrooper, radio operator, and trainer for special forces mobile teams. Paul Andrew Ortiz Collection, (AFC/2001/001/84488, Veterans History Project, American Folklife Center, Library of Congress.

6. "Cold War in Alaska: Nike Missile Sites," Project Jukebox, Digital Branch of the University of Alaska Fairbanks Oral History Program, http://jukebox.uaf.edu/site7/akcoldwar, accessed August 31, 2015. See also http://alaskahistoricalsociety.org/cold-war-in-alaska-project-jukebox/, accessed August 31, 2015.

7. Library of Congress, *Voices of War: Stories of Service from the Home Front and the Front Lines* (Washington D.C.: National Geographic Books, 2004).

8. Tom Wiener, *Forever a Soldier: Unforgettable Stories of Wartime Service* (Washington, D.C.: National Geographic Books, 2005).

9. Todd J. Moye, *Freedom Flyers: The Tuskegee Airmen of World War II* (New York, NY: Oxford University Press, 2010).

10. Kim Heikkila, *Sisterhood of War: Minnesota Woman in Vietnam* (St. Paul, MN: Minnesota Historical Society Press, 2011).

Staff Sergeant Joseph A. Beimfohr
 Joseph Arden Beimfohr Collection (AFC/2001/001/54904), Veterans History Project, American Folklife Center, Library of Congress

3 SECONDARY AND POST-SECONDARY EDUCATION

Oral history assignments are increasingly part of secondary and post-secondary education. As a multidisciplinary teaching tool, oral history can be incorporated into secondary education classroom assignments in a variety of subjects. Its post-secondary uses include undergraduate and graduate assignments and uses by graduate students in master's and Ph.D. work. This chapter covers information for secondary and post-secondary uses of oral history as an educational tool. Information in the chapter is based on standard methodology with references to specific materials developed for use of oral history in an educational setting.

Using oral history assignments in an educational setting begins with an understanding of its methodology, ethics, and best practices. To help meet this need, the Oral History Association (OHA), the national organization for oral history practitioners, developed an education committee that is committed to teacher outreach and support. Several of its members recently adapted the OHA *Principles and Best Practices* for use in the classroom. *The Principles and Best Practices for Oral History Education (4-12)* provide a clear, succinct, and easy-to-follow set of guidelines that can serve as a resource both for secondary and post-secondary educators (http://www.oralhistory.org/wp-content/uploads/2014/04/2013).

Oral historians often recommend that a teacher conduct an interview of his or her own, following oral history methodology from beginning to end, before making an oral history assignment. Oral history classes or workshops available through state and local historical societies and libraries offer training opportunities to help with this recommendation. Nationally, the Oral History Association offers a training workshop at its annual meeting each fall, and the Veterans History Project also offers workshops. Regional oral history associations also offer workshops. If workshops are not available locally, several oral history programs offer on-line e-workshops.[1]

Getting to Know the Veteran

Interviewing veterans at both the secondary and post-secondary levels begins with getting to know the person. Drawing on his experience with oral history in the classroom, educator and oral historian Bob Wettemann reminds us this does not necessarily mean that you have to know a veteran personally, but that you should gain some sense of what he or she did during their tenure in uniform before conducting the interview. As he stated, "If the interviewer has some sense of the interviewee's military career, where they served, the unit they served with, what they did, it helps build the sort of rapport that can lead to a more informative and insightful interview."[2]

After a veteran agrees to do an interview, a pre-interview meeting between a veteran and an educator or student is a helpful way to get to know a veteran. This meeting gives the veteran an opportunity to provide information about her background and service record in preparation for an interview. As with the process discussed earlier in this pamphlet for all interviewers, completing a biographical data form, such as the example included in Appendix C, is a useful step for student interviewers.

A pre-interview meeting also provides an opportunity to determine a veteran's capacity and willingness to work with students. Some veterans make this commitment on an ongoing basis, offering to be interviewed as part of regular class assignments. Others may want to work with students on a one-time or limited basis, and some may decide not to participate after discussing what would be involved. Knowing this at the outset helps the educator and students. And if a veteran has questions about the interview process or the types of questions to expect, a pre-interview meeting is a good time to cover them.

Oral History in Secondary Schools

Recording an interview with a narrator can give student interviewers an opportunity to develop in-depth research, speaking, listening, and analytical thinking skills. As student interviewers talk with narrators about their memories, they hear history firsthand from the people who lived it. The History Channel's "Guidelines for Oral History Interviews: Student Workbook," made this point, stating that "conducting an oral history offers students an opportunity to reach out to older generations…in order to learn more about the past."[3] Reading about the Cuban Missile Crisis in a textbook, for example, can help a student understand the national scope of the event, while talking with a grandparent or neighbor who served in a missile silo during the event can bring history home in a new and immediate way. Such connections with the past can encourage greater depth of understanding of events and time periods for students.

Oral history can be incorporated into a variety of classroom settings.[4] Oral history assignments are most commonly used in history, social studies, and English classes, but they are also well suited for use in independent studies, History Day projects, Eagle Scout projects, and in any class where a teacher is looking to excite students with an opportunity to learn about the past from those who lived it. Classroom projects often are tied to the subject matter being studied, as they can bring a local and personal perspective to the national perspective covered by standard reading materials. In doing so, they can help students more fully understand the causes and impacts of given events, exploring what people at the time thought and felt and making connections between those individuals and the events and times of which they were a part. Student interview projects also benefit from having a particular focus. Projects involving veterans can work well in this regard, as interviews typically cover a specific and clearly defined time and set of events in a narrator's life.

Students do not need to be historians or experts in oral history to use and benefit from this research methodology. With guidance from educators, students of all abilities and academic levels can learn to prepare for and record interviews. Student interviewers can work alone or in teams. If working in teams, they often take the roles of interviewer, equipment operator, and note-taker during the interview, but team members participate equally in all interview preparation—helping with the research, writing questions, and training on the recording equipment.

Oral history is a technology-based educational tool. Student access to recording equipment can vary. In some cases, equipment owned by the school is available. Students sometimes use their phones to record or videotape the interview, though teachers will want to make sure the phones have enough space to record a full interview. Internet telephone programs such as Skype are another option. Regardless of the type of equipment used, encourage students to practice with it while preparing for the interview. See Appendix E for general oral history equipment specifications. Many repositories, such as the Veterans History Project, list their own specifications as well.[5]

Teachers and students also need to be aware that recorded oral history interviews are copyrightable documents. Following standard oral history procedures, student interviewers have several options for handling copyright ownership through use of a legal release agreement. A number of models are available for secondary school educators. In *A Guide to Oral History and the Law,* John A. Neuenschwander suggests that the language for legal release agreements for student projects should define the purpose and use of an interview and, if the oral history is not to be given to a repository, should specify the terms of its return to the narrator when the assignment is completed.[6] Students and educators also can explore options for permanent placement of the interviews in a repository. Many educators work with school or local libraries that agree to serve as repositories for the interviews. The Oral History Association pamphlet *Oral History Projects in Your Classroom* contains an example of a legal release agreement to use in this situation.[7] The Veterans History Project also accepts interviews done by students in grades 10 and up; information about the donation process is available on the project's website (http://www.loc.gov/vets/youth-resources.html).[8]

Pre-Interview Steps and Research

After educators have become oriented to the oral history process and have identified narrators who agree to be interviewed, their students can begin their own preparations for the interviews.[9]

The first step is to formally invite the narrator to participate in the project, usually done with a letter. Information in the letter should briefly describe the project, name the student interviewer or interviewing team, and suggest possible dates for the interview. This should be followed up with a conversation with the veteran to confirm her willingness to do the interview and to set the day and time. Interviews with family members or close friends often are conducted at their homes; interview arrangements also can be made at the school or via Internet telephone programs.

Student interviewers' preparations begin with research. Information provided by the narrator on the biographical data form is the start of this pre-interview research process. It helps students know what to look for and gives them clues about where to look. For example, a student preparing to do an interview with an Army National Guard veteran may find it helpful to look for information about its work and responsibilities, including its role in conflicts and natural disasters. A check on local or state history sources during the years the veteran served could identify events involving the Guard that may lead to questions for the narrator. Or, to give another example, if a narrator was a member of the Armed Forces during the 1950s, research about changes that resulted from the racial integration of the Armed Forces in 1948 could lead to an interesting series of questions. The changing roles of women in the military from the 1960s forward also could also lead to questions for both men and women narrators who served during those years.

Research is critical; a student interviewer's lack of familiarity with the events of specific time periods can lead to miscommunication or a lack of understandings between narrator and interviewer. A student interviewer, for example, might be confused about the meaning and importance of such common Cold War terms as the Iron Curtain, USSR or Soviet Union, Strategic Air Command (SAC), Ground Zero, Atlas or Minuteman or Nike missiles, nuclear arms race, McCarthyism, Berlin Wall, Bay of Pigs, or the Cuban Missile Crisis. With some background research by the student into the time period in which the veteran served, period-specific references by a narrator could open up exciting new areas of discussion.

Conducting this research also gives students valuable experience in working with primary and secondary sources. These sources may be found in school and local libraries, local historical societies, local or state veterans' museums, and directed Internet research. Discussions with librarians, either as a class or individually, can be helpful. Students can also benefit from reading transcripts of finished oral histories, especially those done by other students for classroom projects. Even if the themes and topics of those interviews are not veteran-related, they can lead to classroom discussions about how the kinds of research that appears to be most helpful, how to use the research, the kinds of questions seem to work or not work, and how to structure and pace an interview.

As they conduct their research, encourage students to jot down ideas for questions that they might include in a question guide. For example, if the purpose of an interview is to learn more about serving at a Cold War Atlas missile site, newspaper articles, maps, and photographs may suggest specific questions about where the site was located and how it was operated. Textbooks and other secondary sources also could provide information about events of national significance during the period the narrator was assigned to the site that might open up areas of discussion, such as whether they were placed on high alert during the Cuban missile crisis and what that was like. If letters or diaries from other people stationed at such sites are available, those can offer insight into the daily lives of people assigned to the veteran's site. Once the research is completed, students can review their question ideas and prepare a question guide, discussed next.

A question guide is a written list of the questions and topics that interviewers develop to use during an oral history interview. When developing question guides for an interview with a veteran, students should be encouraged to think about the veteran's experience in the military from its beginning to its end. A veteran's experience begins when he enters the Service, either by enlisting or being drafted. Questions about how and when the veteran entered the Service are a good way to begin a question guide for an interview with a veteran.

Student Interviewer Question Guide

A veteran's experience during the years she served in the military is typically the main focus of an interview with a veteran. Topics for questions students might ask a veteran about this period in her life include the following:

- daily life in the Service
- provision of basic needs—food, clothing, and shelter
- friendships
- interactions between officers and enlisted personnel
- training opportunities
- camp assignments
- camp life

- work assignments
- deployments
- free time and fun
- connections with families at home
- favorite stories

Educators and student interviewers will want to decide which topics from a list like this can best help a student achieve the purpose of the interview and the class assignment. The next step is to organize the questions into themes and topics to be covered in the interview. Common main themes for interviews with veterans include the following:

- Entrance into the Service
- Basic Training and Other Training Opportunities
- Camp Assignments
- Deployment to Combat Zones
- Discharge and Coming Home

These main themes provide a basic structure for the interview. Sending a list like this to the narrator can also help her prepare for the interview.

After the main interview themes have been chosen, identify topics and questions for each. Topics include details to cover about the themes, such as asking about camp life as a specific focus for the Camp Assignments theme. Questions about camp life can cover clothing, barracks life, food, work assignments, and friendships. Write out questions, remembering to use a neutral, open-ended approach. Neutral questions do not anticipate the direction an answer can take. Open-ended questions cannot be answered with "yes" or "no." Examples of each are:

Open-ended question:
Why did you serve in the [branch of the Armed Forces]?

Neutral question:
What did you think about options for Officer Candidate School (OCS) when you joined the military?

The question guide also should include ideas for follow-up questions. Here are some general examples:

What was this about?
What was it like for you?
Why do you think this happened?
I don't understand this information. Can you explain it a little further?

Don't forget to ask about the end of the veteran's time in the Service. The last questions about the narrators' years in the Service usually are about his discharge and coming home. Asking about the trip home, reintegration into family life, and a brief description of his later career can add interesting new information to the discussion.

The final questions on an interview guide are the reflection questions. These questions are designed to encourage narrators to talk about their current thoughts about the information disclosed in the interview. The following are common reflection questions:

> *Looking back, what do you think about your years in the Service?*
> *Is there anything you would have done differently? If so, what and why?*
> *What are your proudest accomplishments and why?*
> *What are your happiest or saddest memories and why?*
> *What would you like young people serving, or thinking of serving, in the military today to know?*

If the veteran served in a combat zone, questions about that period in his life, which can bring up traumatic memories, will have to be handled with care and respect for his emotions. Information about his experiences can provide a depth of insight often not available from other sources, but talking about the events can stir up intense feelings and reactions. The opportunity for the educator to get to know the veteran during pre-interview screening can be helpful in this situation; it offers the chance to discuss possible areas that may be difficult for veterans to discuss with students and can give the educator an opening to ask about how the veteran recommends handling the possibility of dealing with traumatic memories. Classroom preparation when working with persons with traumatic memories can include a discussion of appropriate interview topics and how to respond if a narrator becomes emotional during the interview. Some educators bring a trauma therapist in to the class to help with this preparation.

The Interview

Student interviewers usually interview narrators at the narrator's home or at convenient and accessible pre-arranged location. Depending on the assignment or situation, they may interview veterans in teams or one-on-one. Student interviewers should remember to arrive on time, neatly dressed, with the interview guide printed out and ready to use. Upon their arrival, they should set up the recording equipment, take out paper and pen for note-taking, and review the legal release agreement with the narrator, reminding him they will ask for his signature at the end of the interview and that they will sign it as well.

The interview begins with the interviewer reading aloud a prepared introductory statement that identifies all participants by name and states the purpose, date, and place of the interview. The interviewer can then begin to ask the prepared questions, starting at the beginning of the narrator's story in the military.

Asking questions in an oral history interview is an art. The following tips, summarized from the earlier discussion in this pamphlet, can help the interview go smoothly:

- Ask open-ended questions or prompts that cannot be answered with a simple "yes" or "no." Open-ended questions invite the long explanations and discussions characteristic of oral history interviews. Such questions typically start with the standard *who, what, where, why, when*, and *how* mentioned above. Other starters may be open-ended prompts such as "Tell me about..." and "Please describe..."

- Ask questions in as neutral form as possible. Neutral questions do not represent or suggest a particular point of view, but encourage narrators to answer in a way that reflects their own beliefs and thoughts.

- Don't worry about silences. Be patient after asking a question; veterans often need time to think about an answer.

- Don't interrupt. Allow the veteran to finish speaking before asking another question.

- Ask only one question at a time. Asking several questions at once confuses the narrator.

- Listen carefully and respectfully. Maintain eye contact and use body language rather than verbal comments to encourage the veteran to continue with an answer. Verbal comments that are common in ordinary conversation, such as "Oh," "I see," and "Really," are distracting when listening to the recording or reading the transcript.

- Be prepared to use the information gathered during your research to help the veteran fill in any momentary memory lapse regarding a particular name, date, or place that might occur.

- Ask the veteran to explain unfamiliar military jargon or terminology.

- If using photographs as memory aids, ask the narrator to describe and explain each one. This provides documentation about each photograph directly from the veteran.

- Watch for signs of fatigue in the narrator. Interviews usually last from thirty to ninety minutes and many often run sixty or ninety minutes. Taking a short break every thirty to forty-five minutes is a good rule of thumb.

When the final questions have been asked and answered, the interviewer and narrator sign two copies of the legal release agreement. One copy is kept with the interview materials and a second copy is given to the narrator. The interviewers pack up the recording equipment, take a picture of the veteran in the interview setting, and thank the narrator for the gift of her memories. Within several days, this should be followed with a written thank-you letter.

After the Interview

Final disposition of the interview is guided by the information in the legal release agreement. If, after completion of the assignment, the interview is to be returned to the narrator, the student interviewer should do this. If, however, the oral histories are to be given to a museum or library, gather all materials (the recording, transcript or index, correspondence, biographical data form, signed legal release agreement, and a copy of the question guide), make sure everything is clearly labeled, and send it to the designated repository.

In addition to the interviews, oral history assignments also can include journaling about the process and interview information, writing assignments analyzing the interview information, and developing and presenting class presentations, to name just a few. Any of these options give students an opportunity to reflect on the interview process, the interview itself, and the meaning of the interview information. Thinking about what was said, what it may mean, and how oral histories can provide a close-up human perspective on national or international events helps student interviewers analyze what they hear in the interviews.[10]

Evaluation

Educator's classroom evaluation or assessment materials, designed to document student achievement at the conclusion of an assignment, are available in many oral history education publications. Assessment materials usually include a review of the clarity of interview focus, interviewing style, interview content, and sound quality. If the assignment includes developing a transcript or an index of the recording, the evaluation generally includes the accuracy and overall presentation style of that work as well.[11]

Oral history assignments take time and planning, but the benefits to the students are many. Oral historian and educator Linda Wood has summed up the value of classroom oral history projects in this way, "One of the most important lessons the student learns is that individuals are part of the greater society, and that the individual is shaped by society and in turn helps to shape society. The students get a snapshot of another person's life as it interacts with events outside that life. They learn how the individual reacts to the events, learns from them, and attempts to exert control over what they saw, what they did, and what they thought about the things that they were experiencing. The students listen and learn from these interviews. They learn that history is assembled from these human pieces, that no one piece is less important than any other piece, and that they have a role in making sure the pieces are not lost."[12]

Oral History in Post-Secondary Education

Many of the guidelines offered for students working with veterans on secondary school classroom assignments also apply to the use of oral history in undergraduate and graduate studies. As with secondary students, post-secondary students engaging in oral history projects should both familiarize themselves with basic oral history methodology prior to recording interviews and should get to know each veteran narrator early in the interview process. As described above and elsewhere in this pamphlet, the methodology addresses how to contact narrators, determine a focus and purpose for an interview, do background research and preparation, develop a question guide, decide on recording equipment, identify a possible repository for the interview, develop a legal release agreement, conduct and record the interview, develop an index or transcript of the interview, and submit all materials to the repository. Participating in an oral history interview training session, either in a classroom setting or a workshop, can help ground a student in this methodology.

In post-secondary settings, opportunities for oral history training are somewhat varied. They may be offered as part of the class for which the assignment is made, through other departments at the institution, or by outside organizations. Local or state historical societies, the Oral History Association, regional oral history associations, and the Veterans History Project offer training courses or workshops. On-line courses also are an option. Another helpful resource is the oral history discussion network, H-Oralhist, which includes searchable discussions, reviews, media, links, and blogs related to the practice of oral history.[13] The bottom line is— become familiar with the methodology before beginning the interviews.

An important aspect of oral history methodology includes dealing with the legal status of the interviews. As copyrightable documents, ownership of the intellectual property in an interview must be settled before the interview information may be used. This is handled through a legal release agreement. The most common type of agreement transfers copyright to a designated entity, but oral historians also use Creative

Commons attribution and placement of an interview in the public domain. For more information, see the second edition of *A Guide to Oral History and the Law*.[14]

Plans for ongoing preservation and access of the oral history also are part of basic oral history methodology. Repository options for oral history interviews done by undergraduate and graduate student interviewers with veterans may include the college or university library or archive, historical societies, veterans' museums, and the Veterans History Project. Many post-secondary institutions contain collections of interviews with veterans in their libraries and archives. Some develop formal Veterans History Project programs, such as the Samuel Proctor Oral History Program at the University of Florida.[15] Others are willing to add the work of individual interviewers to their collections.

Institutional Review Board

For several decades, post-secondary students conducting oral histories had to be aware of their institution's Institutional Review Board (IRB) requirements regarding human subjects research. On September 8, 2015, the U.S. Department of Health and Human Services issued a set of recommended revisions to the regulations. Specifically, it recommended that oral history be explicitly excluded from review by institutional review boards, alluding to the fact that oral history already has its own code of ethics, including the principle of informed consent. For continued up-to-date information, see the Oral History Association website (http://www.oralhistory.org/).

Interview Preparation

The oral history process begins with defining the purpose for recording an oral history. Even if its obvious purpose is to fulfill a class assignment, developing a focused purpose statement at the outset helps guide the preparation and interview process.

As with all such interviews, contacting possible narrators with a request for an interview is another important step. Most people asked to participate in an oral history are willing to be interviewed, but a letter formally requesting their involvement demonstrates respect for their potential contribution and underlines the serious purpose of the project. After a narrator has agreed to be interviewed—and some may not be willing—getting to know more about his background is the next step. For veterans, this includes learning about their service record and the years they were in the Service. Taking this time reflects respect for the narrator—in this case a veteran—and her experiences, begins the interview preparation process, and helps build trust and rapport that will carry over into the interview.

This process of getting to know the veteran often involves a pre-interview meeting, either in person or by telephone. A biographical data form, such as that in Appendix C, can serve as a helpful guide for this conversation. Documenting facts about the veteran's years of service provides a starting point for further pre-interview research. It also offers an opportunity to identify any memories that may be sensitive or difficult for the veteran, including any that may be related to PTSD (post-traumatic stress syndrome). For background on handling PTSD in an interview, see the discussion in Chapter Two.

Based on the background information provided by the narrator, the post-secondary interviewer should next seek out additional relevant information in local and state historical societies, local public and research libraries, veterans' museums, and other repositories holding primary and secondary sources. Large, searchable on-line collections such as the Veterans History Project can be excellent resources. This research lays the groundwork for the interview by identifying information already on the record, current gaps in knowledge, and possible topics for interview questions.

Depending on the type of project or assignment, post-secondary students conducting oral histories may find themselves conducting a series of interviews with different people. A strength of oral history is the possibility of seeking out narrators with different backgrounds and perspectives in order to document as broad a range of viewpoints as possible. This can be especially interesting with veterans—a well-defined group of people who represent a wide range of views and ideas about their time in the Service. Interviewing more than one person about the interview purpose, exploring the similarities and differences in their views, can uncover fascinating topics and insights.

Interview Guide

Interview guides are just that—lists of questions an interviewer has prepared to help guide an interview. Interviewers should draw on their research to develop the questions and then organize those questions into main themes and topics to be covered in the interview. Arranging questions this way can help provide organization and structure to an interview. Grouping similar questions together gives the interviewer and narrator an opportunity to explore a topic in some depth. Organizing questions by themes and topics also can help an interviewer pace the interview so as to have adequate time to cover all the main points. Interviewers often share the themes and topics with the narrator to help him prepare for the interview.

Interview guide questions do not need to be written out in full. Many interviewers use keywords or phrases on the interview guide and then formulate specific questions during the interview. This allows them to adapt to the flow of the interview and the particular narrator's style of remembering and to make smooth transitions when asking questions, building on discussions during the interview. Questions and follow-up questions should draw on details identified during pre-interview research to elicit memories from the narrator.

The Interview

Students may think of an oral history as "theirs," but it is important for them to remember that interviews are co-created documents. In an interview, an interviewer and a narrator jointly participate in deciding on the topics to discuss and the information to cover and, until a legal release agreement is signed, both control access to the interview content. In addition, oral history ethics and best practices remind interviewers not to surprise narrators with trick questions, ask leading or value-laden questions, or record narrators without their knowledge.

Oral history interviews should begin with the interviewer reading a prepared written introduction identifying each participant, the purpose of the interview, and when and where the interview is being recorded. The opening questions should encourage the narrator to start his story at the beginning of his connection to the purpose of the interview—in this case, entrance into the Armed Forces. Questions about entering military service are usually asked first, as that is where a narrator's story as a veteran started. The interviewer then guides the narrator through the interview topics and questions. Many narrators remember things in chronological order, and thus arranging topics and questions in this order is usually most effective. The final questions ask the narrator to discuss his current thoughts and insights about the memories just discussed.

After the Interview

After completing the interview, interviewers start the final oral history steps, which frequently include developing either an index to the interview content or a transcript. If the oral histories are to be given to a repository, all materials are compiled and turned in. With this step, the student interviewer has added unique new information to the historical record.

Collections of interviews with veterans conducted and preserved at post-secondary institutions have recently expanded to include organized projects with student veterans. The stated purpose of one such project, From Combat to Kentucky: Student Veteran Oral History Project (C2KY), is to conduct interviews with veterans of Operation Iraqi Freedom and Operation Enduring Freedom in Afghanistan who are students pursuing post-secondary education in Kentucky.[16] Rather than waiting to talk with veterans about their memories related to military service until later in their lives, these projects offer veterans an opportunity to discuss and preserve those experiences while they are still relatively fresh in their minds. The interviews provide new insights into the post-military paths of veterans engaged in educational opportunities made available to them through their Service, information that adds to our understanding of the experiences of veterans in the United States. To sum up, in the words of Mary Marshall Clark, co-director of the Oral History Master of Arts program at Columbia University, "The great strength of oral history is its ability to record memories in a way that honors the dignity and integrity of ordinary people."[17]

References

1. For more information about workshops, contact your local or state historical society or local library. See the Oral History Association for information about training opportunities at the annual meeting and for links to regional oral history associations. http://www.oralhistory.org/resources/, accessed August 23, 2015. See also the Veterans History Project, "How to Participate in the Project," http://www.loc.gov/vets/kit.html, accessed August 23, 2015. For an example of online resources, see the "Workshop on the Web," an e-workshop offered by the Baylor Institute for Oral History, http://www.baylor.edu/oralhistory/index.php?id=23560, accessed August 23, 2015. The online Quiz for Educators from the Institute covers many of the frequently asked questions that teachers face when working with oral history in the classroom. See "Oral History Workshop for Teachers Quiz" at http://www.baylor.edu/content/services/document.php/134967.pdf, accessed August 23, 2015.

2. Email from Robert P. Wettemann, Jr., CTR USAF USAFA USAFA/DFH, Director of the United States Air Force Academy Center for Oral History, to Barbara Sommer, July 23, 2015.

3. "Guidelines for Oral History Interviews: Student Workbook," The History Channel, http://www.history.com/images/media/interactives/oralhistguidelines.pdf, accessed August 23, 2015. See also Cliff Kuhn, Marjorie L. McLellan Rich Nixon, Susan Moon, and Toby Daspit, "Voices of Experience: Oral History in the Classroom" in *Preparing the Next Generation of Oral Historians*, edited by Barry A. Lanman and Laura W. Wendling (Lanham, MD: AltaMira Press, 2006), 33-53. See also Barry A. Lanman, "The Oral History Experience: A Model for the Use of Oral History in Education" in the same volume, 55-84. And for further information, see the following: Glenn Whitman, *Dialogue with the Past: Engaging Students & Meeting Standards through Oral History* (Walnut Creek, CA: AltaMira Press, 2004). The Veterans History Project Student Edition, http://vhpstudentedition.org/, accessed September 6, 2015. "Veterans' Stories: The Veterans History Project," Teacher's Guide: Primary Source Set, Library of Congress Teaching With Primary Sources, http://www.loc.gov/teachers/classroommaterials/primarysourcesets/veterans/pdf/teacher_guide.pdf, accessed September 8, 2015.

4. For additional discussion on meeting educator goals, see Glenn Whitman, *Dialogue with the Past: Engaging Students & Meeting Standards through Oral History* (Walnut Creek, CA: AltaMira Press, 2004).

5. See "Accepted Media and Format Standards," *Veterans History Project Field Kit*, 13, http://www.loc.gov/vets/pdf/fieldkit-2013.pdf, accessed August 23, 2015.

6. John A. Neuenschwander, "Form 11. Permission to Use: Middle & High School," *A Guide to Oral History and the Law, 2nd ed.* (New York, NY: Oxford University Press, 2014), 127-128.

7. Linda Wood, *Oral History Projects in Your Classroom* (Oral History Association, 2001), 73.

8. For more information, see The Veterans History Project, "How to Participate: Especially for Educators and Students," http://www.loc.gov/vets/youth-resources.html, accessed August 23, 2015.

9. See the "Pre-Interview" page of the OHA *Principles and Best Practices for Oral History Education* (4-12), http://www.oralhistory.org/wp-content/uploads/2014/04/2013-1411_Oral_History_ClassroomGuide_Update_V2.pdf, accessed August 23, 2015. See also "Guidelines for Oral History Interviews: The History Channel," http://www.history.com/images/media/interactives/oralhistguidelines.pdf, accessed August 23,2015.

10. For examples of secondary school student analysis materials, see Glenn Whitman, *Dialogue with the Past: Engaging Students & Meeting Standards through Oral History* (Walnut Creek, CA: AltaMira Press, 2004), 137-140.

11. See "Handouts and Reproducible Forms" in Linda Wood, Oral History Projects in Your Classroom (Oral History Association, 2001), 59-87. See also "Resources for the Oral History Educator" in Barry A. Lanman and Laura M. Wendling, *Preparing the Next Generation of Oral Historians: An Anthology of Oral History Education* (Lanham, MD: AltaMira Press, 2006), 425-448. Glenn Whitman, *Dialogue with the Past: Engaging Students & Meeting Standards through Oral History* (Walnut Creek, CA: AltaMira Press, 2004), 109-155.

12. Linda Wood, *Oral History Projects in Your Classroom* (Oral History Association, 2001), 55.

13. For more information, see the Oral History Association at http://www.oralhistory.org/resources/, accessed August 27, 2015, the Veterans History Project at http://www.loc.gov/vets/workshopinfo.html, accessed August 27, 2015, and H-Oralhist at https://networks.h-net.org/h-oralhist, accessed August 27, 2015.

14. John A. Neuenschwander, *A Guide to Oral History and the Law, 2nd ed.* (New York, NY: Oxford University Press, 2014). See also Barbara W. Sommer, *Practicing Oral History in Historical Organizations* (Walnut Creek, CA: Left Coast Press, Inc., 2015).

15. For more information, see the Samuel Proctor Oral History Program, Veterans History Project, http://oral.history.ufl.edu/projects/vhp/, accessed August 27, 2015.

16. "From Combat to Kentucky: Student Veteran Oral History Project," Louie B Nunn Center for Oral History, University of Kentucky Libraries, http://www.kentuckyoralhistory.org/series/18984/combat-kentucky-student-veteran-oral-history-project, accessed August 25, 2015. See also the Student Veteran Oral History Project at Monmouth University in New Jersey, http://library.monmouth.edu/main/content/student-veteran-oral-history-project, accessed August 25, 2014.

17. Quoted on webpage of Oral History Master of Arts, Columbia University, New York City, http://oralhistory.columbia.edu/, accessed August 27, 2015.

First Lieutenant Mary L. Weiss Hester
Mary L. Weiss Hester Collection (AFC/2001/001/32449), Veterans History Project, American Folklife Center, Library of Congress

These appendices include examples of forms, guidelines, additional interviewing tips, equipment standards, and other materials developed for oral history interviewers of veterans. Sources are listed; interviewers are encouraged to review the source materials for further information and guidelines.

APPENDIX A: Best Practices for Community Oral Historians

In addition to the Oral History Association Principles and Best Practices discussed in this pamphlet, the following list of ten best practices was developed specifically for oral historians working in a community setting. They emphasize the ethics and integrity that the Oral History Association materials stress and also focus on actions that can help guide community involvement and community relations.

1. **Familiarize yourself with the Oral History Association's guidelines.** First developed in 1968 and revised and updated regularly, these guide the practice of ethical oral history and form the foundation on which solid oral history projects are built. Becoming familiar with them will help your project get off to a strong start.

2. **Focus on oral history as a process.** Using standard historical research methods, you are setting out to explore a historical question through recorded interviews, giving them context and preserving them in the public record—in addition to whatever short-term goals your project may have, such as using interview excerpts to create an exhibit or celebrate an anniversary.

3. **Cast a wide net to include community.** Make sure all appropriate community members are involved in your project and have an opportunity to make a contribution. Community members know and care the most about the project at hand, and the more closely they are involved in every aspect of it, the more successful it will be.

4. **Understand the ethical and legal ramifications of oral history.** Oral historians record deeply personal stories that become available in an archive for access both in the present and the future. So oral historians have ethical and legal responsibilities to abide by copyright laws and respect narrators' wishes while also being true to the purposes of oral history.

5. **Make a plan.** At the outset, define your purpose, set goals, evaluate your progress, and establish record-keeping systems so details don't get out of control.

6. **Choose appropriate technology with an eye toward present and future needs.** Technology is necessary for recording interviews, preserving them in an archive, and providing access and using them for public displays. Make wise decisions about the technology you use.

7. **Train interviewers and other project participants to assure consistent quality.** Oral history interviews differ from some other interview-based research methods in the amount of background research and preparation required. Make sure interviewers and other personnel are thoroughly trained in oral history principles, interviewing techniques, recording technology and ethics.

8. **Conduct interviews that will stand the test of time.** This is the heart of the oral history process, but its success depends on laying solid groundwork.

9. **Process and archive all interview materials to preserve them for future use.** Oral history interviews and related materials should be preserved, catalogued and made available for others to use in a suitable repository, such as a library, archive or historical society.

10. **Take pride in your contribution to the historical record.** Share with the community what you've learned, and celebrate your success.

Mary Kay Quinlan, Nancy MacKay, and Barbara W. Sommer, *Introduction to Community Oral History: Community Oral History Toolkit*, Volume 1. (Walnut Creek, CA: Left Coast Press, Inc., 2013):12-13.

APPENDIX B: Example of a Legal Release Agreement

LEGAL RELEASE AGREEMENT

The purpose of this oral history interview is to document your experiences and memories. Please read and sign this gift agreement so your interview will be available for future use.

AGREEMENT I, _____ , narrator, donate and convey my oral history interview dated _____ to the _____ (oral history project/repository name). In making this gift I understand that I am conveying all right, title, and interest in copyright to the oral history project/repository. I also grant the oral history project/repository the right to use my name and likeness in promotional materials for outreach and educational materials. In return, the oral history project/repository grants me a non-exclusive license to use my interview through my lifetime. I further understand that I will have the opportunity to review and approve my interview before it is placed in the repository and made available to the public. Once I have approved it, the oral history project/repository will make my interview available for research without restriction. Future uses may include quotation in printed materials or audio/video excerpts in any media, and availability on the Internet.

NARRATOR NAME (print) _____

Signature _____ Date _____

INTERVIEWER NAME (print) _____

Signature _____ Date _____

SPECIAL CONDITIONS OR COMMENTS:

Source: This form is adapted from the "Sample Forms for Managing Projects," Nancy MacKay, Mary Kay Quinlan, *Community Oral History Toolkit,* 2013, http://www.lcoastpress.com/book.php?id=404. For additional examples, see John A. Neuenschwander, *A Guide to Oral History and the Law,* 2nd ed. (New York, NY: Oxford University Press, 2014).

BIOGRAPHICAL DATA FORM

Use reverse or additional sheet if service was in more than one war or conflict.
PLEASE PRINT CLEARLY

<u>Narrator Information</u>

Veteran ❑ Civilian ❑ _____
first   middle   last

_____
maiden name, nickname, other names known by – identify each

Address: City State ZIP _____

_____

Telephone-Area Code and Number: _____ Email Address_____

Place of Birth _____ Birth Date _____
month/day/year

Race/Ethnicity (optional) _____Male ❑ Female ❑

Branch of Service or Wartime Activity _____

Commissioned ❑ Enlisted ❑ Drafted ❑ Service dates _____to _____

Highest Rank _____

Unit, Division, Battalion, Group, Ship, etc. (Do not abbreviate) _____

_____

War, operation, or conflict served in (list each with dates served) _____

_____

Locations of military or civilian service (list each with dates served) _____

_____

Battles/campaigns (list each with dates served) _____

_____

APPENDIX C: Sample Forms

Medals or special service awards. (list each, be as specific as possible) _____

_____

Special duties/highlights/achievements (list and be specific) _____

_____

Prisoner of War? Yes ❑ No ❑ (places and dates) _____

Combat or service-related injuries? Yes ❑ No ❑

Additional Biographical Information:

Have you documented your Service in the past? If so, list the details here_____

_____

Do you have letters, diaries, photographs, maps, military manuals, yearbooks, medals, uniforms or other

materials concerning your service as a veteran? Yes ❑ No ❑

<u>Interviewer Information</u> (fill in all applicable information)

Veteran ❏ Civilian ❏ _____
                   first   middle   last

                              _____
                           maiden name, nickname, other names known by – identify each

Address: City State ZIP _____

                                  _____

Telephone-Area Code and Number: _____ Email Address_____

Place of Birth _____ Birth Date _____
                                                      month/day/year

Race/Ethnicity *(optional)* _____Male ❏ Female ❏

Branch of Service or Wartime Activity _____

Commissioned ❏ Enlisted ❏ Drafted ❏ Service dates _____to _____

Highest Rank _____

Unit, Division, Battalion, Group, Ship, etc. (Do not abbreviate) _____

_____

War, operation, or conflict served in (list each with dates served) _____

_____

Locations of military or civilian service (list each with dates served) _____

_____

Battles/campaigns (list each with dates served) _____

_____

Medals or special service awards. (list each, be as specific as possible) _____

_____

APPENDIX C: Sample Forms

Special duties/highlights/achievements (list and be specific) _____

_____

Prisoner of War? Yes ❑ No ❑ (places and dates) _____

Combat or service-related injuries? Yes ❑ No ❑

Additional Biographical Information:

Have you documented your service? If so, list the details here_____

_____

Source: Form is adapted from the Veterans History Project "Biographical Data Form," Veterans History Project *Field Kit*, pp. 5-6, http://www.loc.gov/vets/pdf/biodata-fieldkit-2013.pdf and the Wisconsin Veterans Museum – Research Center, "Oral History Interview Request," http://www.wisvetsmuseum.com/uploads/PDFs/8-1-2-1%20Oral%20History%20Interview%20Request%20Form.pdf, accessed August 28, 2015.

Interview Summary Form

PROJECT NAME (if applicable) _____

NARRATOR (full name as it will appear on all records related to this interview:

OTHER NAMES KNOWN BY (including nicknames) _____

ADDRESS: _____

_____

BIRTH PLACE AND DATE_____

TELEPHONE, including Area Code_____ ____ E-MAIL _____

INTERVIEWER (full name as it will appear on all records related to the interview)

_____

ADDRESS _____

_____

TELEPHONE, including Area Code_____ EMAIL_____

INTERVIEW PLACE _____

INTERVIEW DATE _____ INTERVIEW LENGTH _____

RECORDING MEDIUM _____ digital audio _____digital video

VIDEO type ❑ Digital Video (MiniDV, DVCAM, DVPRO) ❑DVD-R Video ❑Flash Drive ≤ Flash Drive ❑

Other _____
     (identify)

AUDIO type: Cassette ❑ CD-R ❑ Flash Drive ❑

DIGITAL FILE type ❑WAV ❑MPEG2 ❑MPEG4/H.264 ❑TXT/RTF ❑TIF/JPG

DELIVERY MEDIUM _____sound file _____sound card ____ CD _____DVD _____ flash drive

DATE LEGAL RELEASE AGREEMENT SIGNED _____

APPENDIX C: Sample Forms

TECHNICAL NOTES (make/model of recorder, format recorded, microphone notes)

BRIEF INTERVIEW NOTES (physical environment, recording sound environment)

LIST OF PROPER NAMES (personal and place names with proper spelling)

SUMMARY OF INTERVIEW CONTENT (brief description of interview content in sequence)
Example: 00:00 Introduction
           01:45 Enlisted
           03:25 Chose branch of service and why

FORM COMPLETED BY _____ DATE_____

Source: Form adapted from "Interview Summary," MacKay, Quinlan, Sommer, *Community Oral History Toolkit,* http://www.lcoastpress.com/book.php?id=404 and the Veterans History Project "Audio and Video Recording Log," Veterans History Project *Field Kit,* pp. 9-10, http://www.loc.gov/vets/pdf/audioviideo-fieldkit-2013.pdf, accessed August 28, 2015.

Photograph/Memorabilia/Artifact Form
Use one form for each item or set of items. Please print clearly.

Project Name (if applicable) _____

Owner's Name _____
                       (as listed on the biographical data form)

Address:_____

_____

Item: _____

Type:_____ Quantity: _____

Detailed Description:

Associated Names and Dates:

Physical Condition:

Instructions for Use:

Disposition:
Returned to Owner by: _____ Date: _____
                            (name)

Deposited in Repository by: _____ Date: _____
                                 (name)

Form Completed by: _____

Address:_____

Signature: _____ Date:_____

Source: Form adapted from the "Photograph & Memorabilia Receipt," MacKay, Quinlan, Sommer, *Community Oral History Toolkit*, http://www.lcoastpress.com/book.php?id=404, accessed August 28, 2015.

APPENDIX D: Sample Correspondence

Interview Contact/Request Letter

Date

Return Address

Dear [name of narrator]

    I am writing this letter to ask you to sit for an oral history interview about your experience as a United States veteran. We are interviewing veterans in our area to document their experiences during their years of service and hope you will consider being part of this effort. I will be doing this interview for the [insert name of organization or institution]. [If working with a team, introduce them here].

    I would like to talk with you about the interview in more detail. I will call you within the week to discuss it further and to answer any questions you may have. I also can be reached at [insert telephone number and email address]

    I am looking forward to talking with you and documenting your military service.

Sincerely yours,

[name]
organization or institution

Interview Confirmation Letter

Date

Return Address

Dear [name of narrator]

Thank you for agreeing to be interviewed about your experiences as a United States veteran. Your interview is scheduled for [insert date and place and time].

During the interview we will cover the following topics [list the topics] Please feel free to add anything you want to include.

We will [audio and video] record your interview. At the end of the interview, we'll ask you to sign our legal release agreement to determine what will happen to it after we record it.

I am looking forward to interviewing you. [If the interviewer is working with a team, include their names here] Please let me know if you have any questions. Here again is my contact information [insert contact information].

Sincerely yours,

[interviewer name]

[name of organization or institution]

APPENDIX D: Sample Correspondence

Thank You Letter

[date]

[return address]

Dear [name of narrator]

Thank you very much for the excellent oral history interview you shared with us about your experiences as a veteran. As we discussed this interview is now [fill in what will happen to the interview]

We've enclosed a copy of your recording [and transcript if one is done] with this letter. Please let me know if you have any questions.

Thank you again.

Sincerely yours,

[name of interviewer]

[name of institution or organization]

Oral History Transmittal Letter

Date

Contributor's Name _____

Organization_____

Address _____

_____

Phone _____Email _____

Dear:

Enclosed, please find recordings for [insert name of veteran]

Materials Enclosed

_____   _____
_____   _____
_____   _____
_____   _____
_____   _____
_____   _____

I have reviewed the following checklist to ensure that each of my collections meets the requirements.

SUBMISSION CHECKLIST

☐ Original, unedited interview/materials ☐ Signed and dated Legal Release Agreement

☐ Recordings last at least 30 minutes ☐ Completed Interview Summary Form

☐ One recording per media format (CD, DVD etc.) ☐ Photograph, Memorabilia, and Artifact Form

☐ Biographical Data Form

Signed,

_____

Adapted from "Cover Letter," Veterans History Project *Field Kit,* p.4, http://www.loc.gov/vets/pdf/coverletter-fieldkit-2013.pdf, accessed August 28, 2015.

APPENDIX E: Equipment Specifications

ACCEPTED MEDIA AND FORMAT STANDARDS
The Library of Congress Veterans History Project

Use the highest-quality recording equipment available to you. The Library of Congress requires that you submit unedited materials in their original format. Recordings must be at least thirty (30) minutes in length. Record only one interview per media. Do not write on, add labels to or copy protect any CD or DVD.

VHP accepts the following media:
 • Digital Video (DV) MiniDV, DVCAM, DVPRO
 • DVD-R Video
 • Audio Cassettes
 • CD-R Audio
 • Flash Drives

Use the following file extensions:
 • WAV on CD-R or a Flash Drive Specifications: 96 kHz, 24-bit (suggested) or 44.1 kHz, 16-bit
 • MPEG-2 on DVD-R or a Flash Drive Specifications: at least 3Mbps, with a spatial resolution of 720x486 at 30fps or the highest your set-up allows.
 • MPEG-4/H.264 on DVD-R or a Flash Drive Specifications: at least 3Mbps, with a spatial resolution of 720x486 at 30fps or the highest your set-up allows.
 • TXT/RFT on CD-R, DVD-R, or a Flash Drive Specifications: 600 dpi (suggested) or 300 dpi
 • TIF/JPG on CD-R, DVD-R, or a Flash Drive Specifications: 600 dpi (suggested) or 300 dpi

"Accepted Media and Format Standards," Veterans History Project *Field Kit,* p. 13, http://www.loc.gov/vets/pdf/mediaformat-fieldkit-2013.pdf, accessed July 17, 2015.

For more information, see Appendix C: "Recording Equipment Standards," Barbara W. Sommer, Nancy MacKay, and Mary Kay Quinlan, *Planning A Community Oral History Project,* vol. 2 of *Community Oral History Toolkit* (Walnut Creek, CA: Left Coast Press, Inc., 2013), 119-124. See also the *Oral History in the Digital Age* website, http://ohda.matrix.msu.edu/.

*NOTE- There is no magic list of questions that covers all types of interviews. This list should only be used as a guide and/or starting point. Personalize and add to these questions taking into account a veteran's branch of service, training, type of work, where they were stationed, the battles they fought in, etc. The best questions come from researching and learning more about the person before going into the interview. Make sure to listen to the narrator and ask appropriate follow-up questions.

Introduction:
Every oral history interview should begin with an introductory statement. Introduce yourself, the veteran, and anybody else who is present in the room (even if they aren't speaking). State where you are, what the date is, and briefly why you are interviewing the veteran.

Demographic and Background:
Tell me when and where you were born?
> Where were you raised? Give us a quick description of the place and the people.

Describe your family.
> Your siblings, your parents?
> Describe your family's ties to the military and military families.

What did you do for fun as a child?
> Tell us a memorable story.

Family life
> Briefly describe your family life.
> Tell us about your chores or responsibilities?
> Describe what you and your family did for fun.

Education - tell me about your elementary, middle, and high schools
> Describe your school including its size and location.
> What were your favorite subjects and why?
> Tell us a couple of memorable stories.

What about after school and summer jobs? Describe yours

Tell us about college or any other post-secondary education you have had?
> What effect did this have on your decision to go into the Service?
> What effect did it have on your military service overall?

Service:
Tell us about going into the Service?
> Were you drafted or enlisted. Describe the experience.
> What do you remember about your recruiter?

Which branch of the Armed Forces were you in and why?

What were your family's reactions to your going into the Service?
> What were your friends' reactions?
> Tell us about your reaction.
>> What was most important to you and why?

Training
Tell me about entering the Service.

Describe the physical and getting your shots.
Describe being sworn in.
Describe boot camp.
Tell us about where you were assigned.
What stands out in your memory about your first days and months in the Service?
What did you learn about military life in boot camp?
Tell us about one or two memorable stories?
Advanced training – describe any advanced training you received?
What did you think about it?

Military Life
Describe your assignments after boot camp, beginning with the first one.
Describe the units you were assigned to
Describe the barracks
Describe the food
Describe the clothes
Tell us about your daily work responsibilities.
Tell us about who you reported to.
Tell us about opportunities to advance in rank or responsibilities.
Describe a day in the life of a soldier
Rules and restrictions - what worked and what didn't?

Friendships and Family
Tell us about your military friends.
When and how did you meet them?
Describe what you did for relaxation in your free time.
On the base?
In town?
Visiting family?
Tell us about being separated from family and communications from home

Combat-Related Assignments
Describe receiving orders for a combat-related assignment.
What was your reaction?
Where were you located or stationed?
Describe training for your assignment.
What stands out in your mind and why?
Describe your assignment (or assignments)
Tell us about how you traveled to the location?
Tell us about your work and your work assignments.
Describe your daily duties and responsibilities.
Tell us about the routines.
Tell us about days or times that were not routine?
What about morale & the morale of others – men and women - on the assignment?
How would you describe it and why?
Describe stress - yours and others
What do you think caused it and why?
How did you and others with you handle it?
Describe your most difficult times.

What stands out in your memory and why?
What are one or two stories that stand out for you and why?
Describe less difficult times
What are one or two memorable stories?
Describe the others serving with you.
What did they mean to you and why?
Describe your correspondence and contacts with family and friends at home
How did it make you feel?
Tell us about what you did to relax?
Describe what you did to have fun?
Describe knowing you would be leaving the combat zone.
Tell us about how you left.
Tell us about interesting or memorable experiences or stories that haven't come up yet and that
you would like to share?

Discharge & Coming Home:
Describe hearing that you were due to be discharged from the Service.
Describe getting ready to leave.
Describe being discharged.
What were your thoughts about this and why?
Describe coming home
Tell us about your trip home.
Describe any family or community celebrations.

Post-Military Service
Describe your reintegration into civilian life.
Tell us about your family's responses to reintegration?
Tell us about your friend's responses to reintegration?
What was it like to go back to work?
Describe your family
Tell us about your family now.
Describe your work and career
Tell us how your work and career
Describe whether or how your military training figured into your current work and
career.
Describe whether or how veterans' education benefits figured into your current work
and career.
What would you say the impact of military life has had on your career and why?
Describe your free time
Tell us about your hobbies, friends, and how you spend your free time.

Veterans Organizations
Describe your involvement in veteran's organizations.
What does they mean to you and why?
Tell us about your participation in events involving veterans such as marching in parades,
helping with military funerals, social contacts, other?
Why do (would) you do this? What are your thoughts about doing this?
Tell us about reunions?
Describe your involvement in them and why.

Describe visiting any of the places you trained or were stationed.
>What was that like for you?

Describe Honor Flights in your area.
>What about your participation?

Describe your use of veteran's benefits.
>What about education benefits? – see question above.
>What about medical benefits?
>What do they mean to you?

Reflections

What were your thoughts about military service at the time you served?
What are your thoughts about your military service now?
How would you describe life lessons learned in the military and why?
What would you recommend to someone considering military service today and why?

Closing:

Before we conclude, is there anything else that you would like to add or stories you would like to share that we didn't get to?

Thank you for your service and taking the time today to share your experiences with me/us.

Source: The State Historical Society of Missouri Oral History Program.

CPSIA information can be obtained
at www.ICGtesting.com
Printed in the USA
LVOW04s1127070917
547883LV00005B/7/P